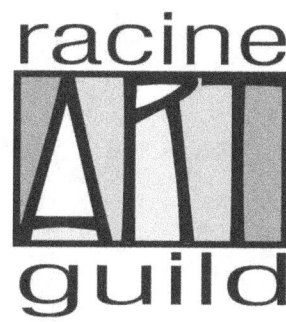

Works of Art
by the Artists of the Racine Art Guild.

The purpose of the Racine Art Guild is to promote creative art for the mutual benefit of members, and to advance the appreciation of art in Racine.

The Racine Art Guild was organized in 1957 and has operated continuously for 60 years.

Membership is open to anyone interested. Individual annual membership dues are $30 for a single or $40 for two adults residing at the same address. Membership dues are payable no later than January 31 to allow the member to be in the membership yearbook. To participate in the Annual Juried Show artists must have current memberships at the time entries are dropped off. Current members will receive the newsletter and be able to sign up for workshops and trips and to participate in the Invitational Show.

Unless otherwise specified, programs are held at Wustum Museum, 2519 Northwestern Avenue, Racine, at 6:00 pm on the second Thursday of the month. Our meetings are at Wustum to support and compliment the programs and exhibitions of this fine art museum, and thereby facilitate our goal of promoting appreciation of arts in the community.

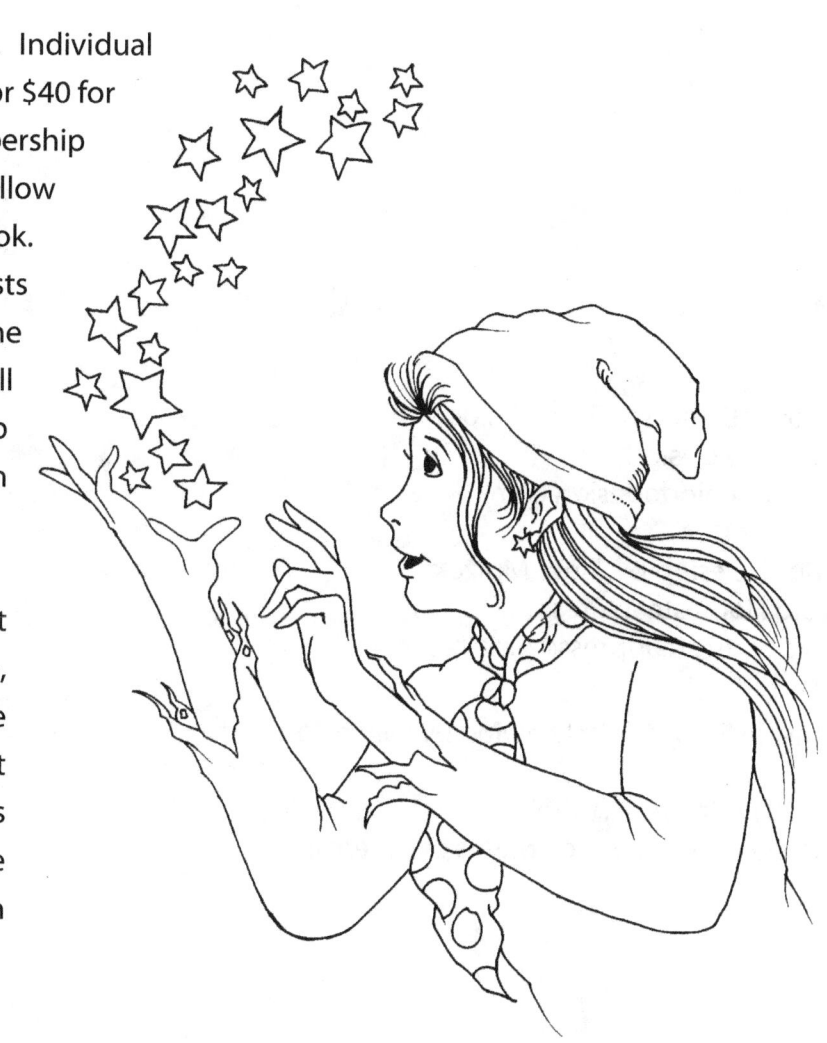

Cover Design by Trace Chiodo
Chiodo Design
http://chiododesign.com

Book Design by Janet Mrazek
Old Homestead Press
oldhomesteadpress@gmail.com

Inside Front Cover Drawing by Lance Raichert

INDEX OF ARTISTS

DEDICATION

The commemorative coloring book created for the 50th Anniversary of the Starving Artist Fair is dedicated to 60 years of leadership of the Racine Art Guild from 1957 until today.

RACINE ART GUILD PAST PRESIDENTS

1957-1958 • Jo Kuhns

1958-1960 • Betty Girtler

1960-1961 • Ester Kaufman

1961-1963 • Helen Rusk

1963-1964 • Jane Beaugrand

1964 -1966 • Connie Barrington

1966-1967 • Bonnie Knop

1967-1969 • Carol Madsen

1969-1971 • Carol Shoemaker

1971-1972 • Mary Zielke

1972-1974 • Eleanor Markusen

1974-1977 • Peg Lukow

1977-1978 • Ilona Willing

1978-1979 • Lorna Hennig

1979-1980 • Barb Purteil &
      Mary Jo Kaiserlian

1981-1982 • Jo Winnen &
      Mary Terselic

1981-1982 • Mary Terselic

1982-1983 • Alice LaBeau

1983-1985 • Loraine Brink

1985-1986 • Mary Bullette

1986-1988 • Alice Schuebel

1988-1989 • Mary Spangler

1989-1990 • Jeanne Rognile

1990-1991 • Sue Sorenson

1991-1992 • Pat Guttenberg

1992-1993 • Alice Hazarian

1993-1994 • Kay McCelland

1994-1996 • Tom Hunt

1996-1997 • Cherie Bell Uhlanhake

1997-1999 • Kay McCelland &
      Janet Mrazek

1999-2000 • Pat Guttenberg

2000 -2001 • Pat Guttenberg &
      Alice Hazarian

2001-2003 • Francis Ziemann

2003-2005 • Kate Proeber

2005-2007 • James Chaplin

2008-2009 • Tom White

2009-2010 • JoAnne Nissen

2011-2012 • Nancy Neider &
      Carolyn Chaplin

2013-2014 • Nancy Neider &
      Pam Kazarian

2015-2016 • Nancy Neider &
      Janet Mrazek

2017-2018 • Jill Castillo &
      Sarah Anderson

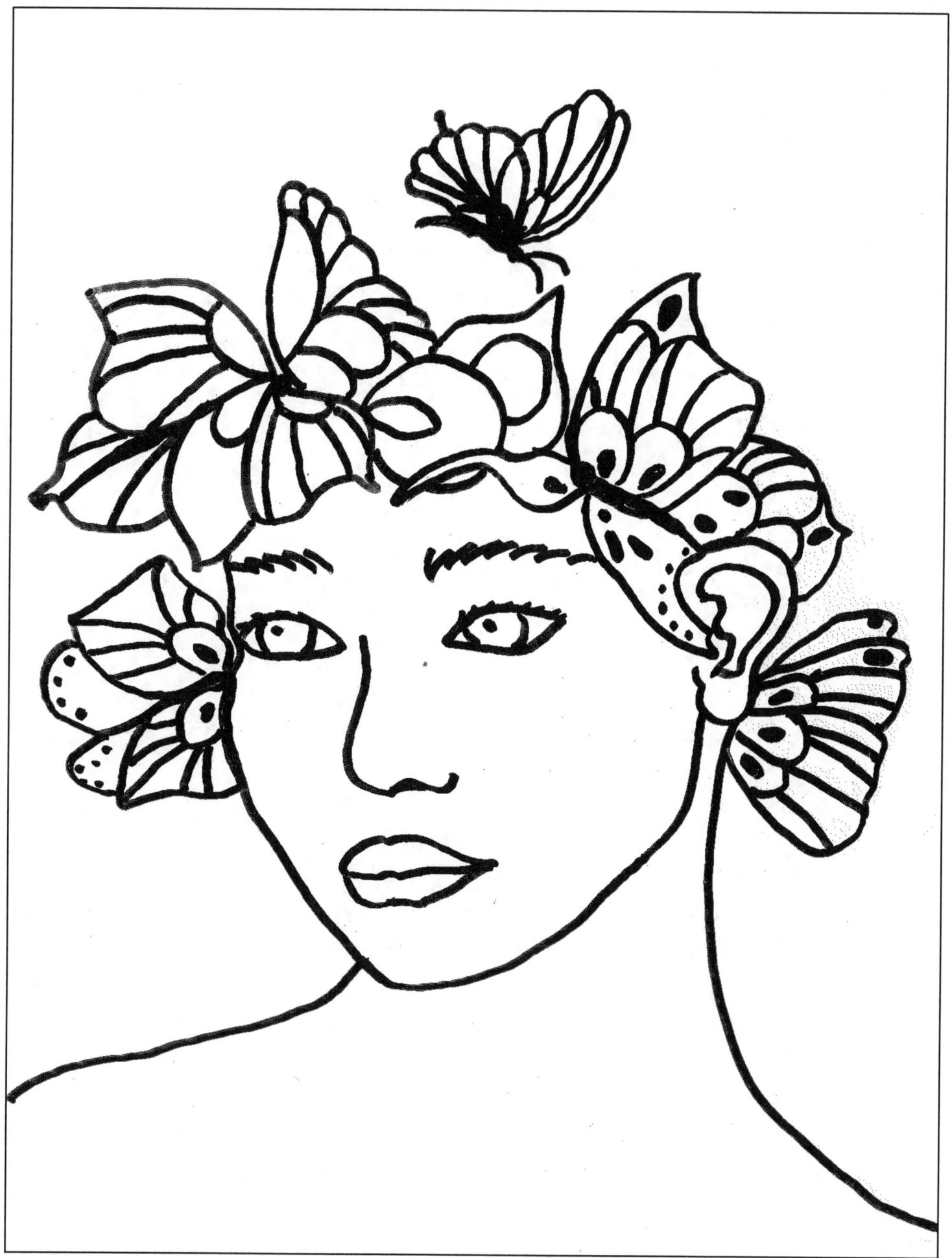

Sue Kadamian

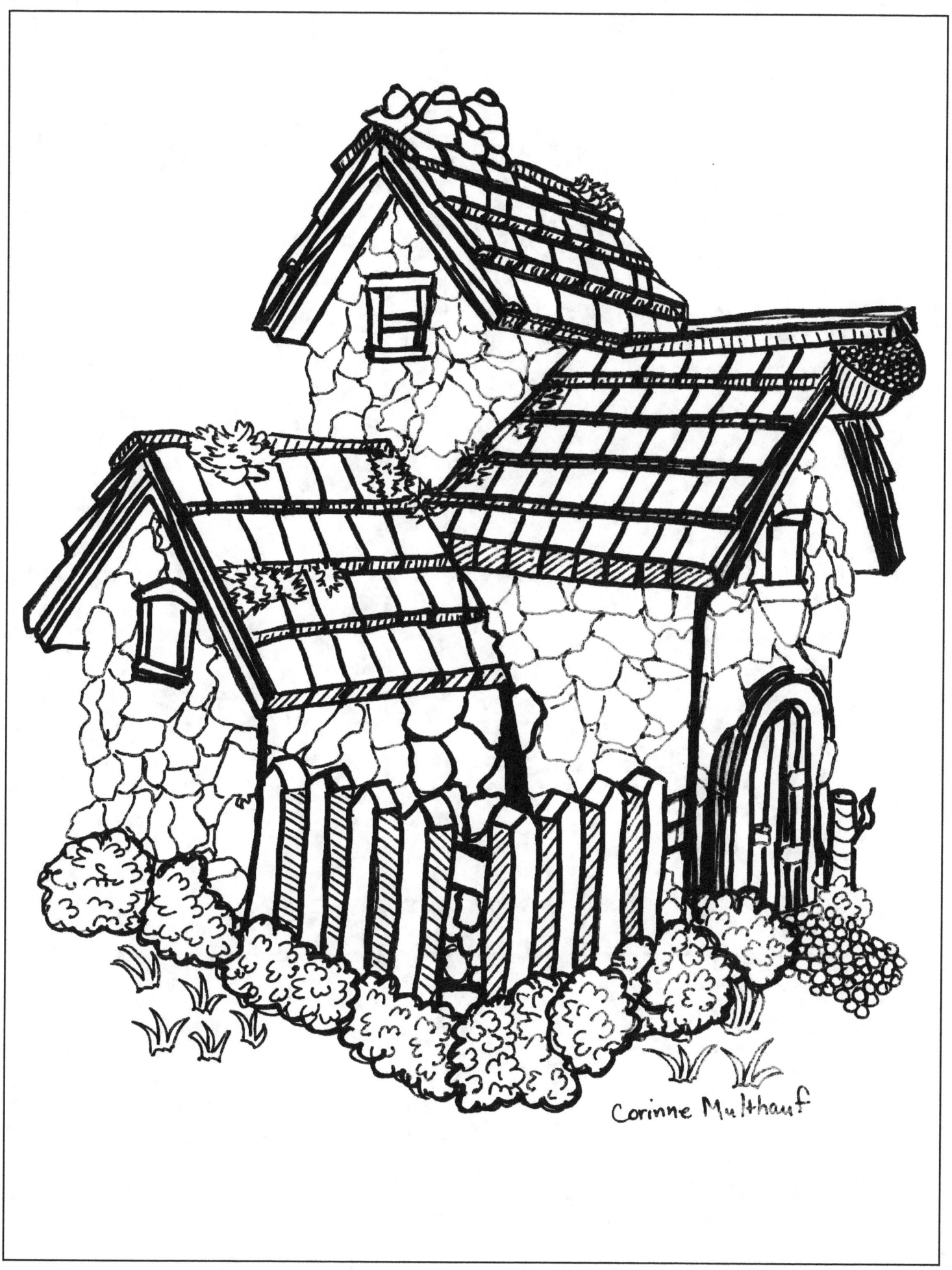

Corinne Multhauf, *Fairy House*

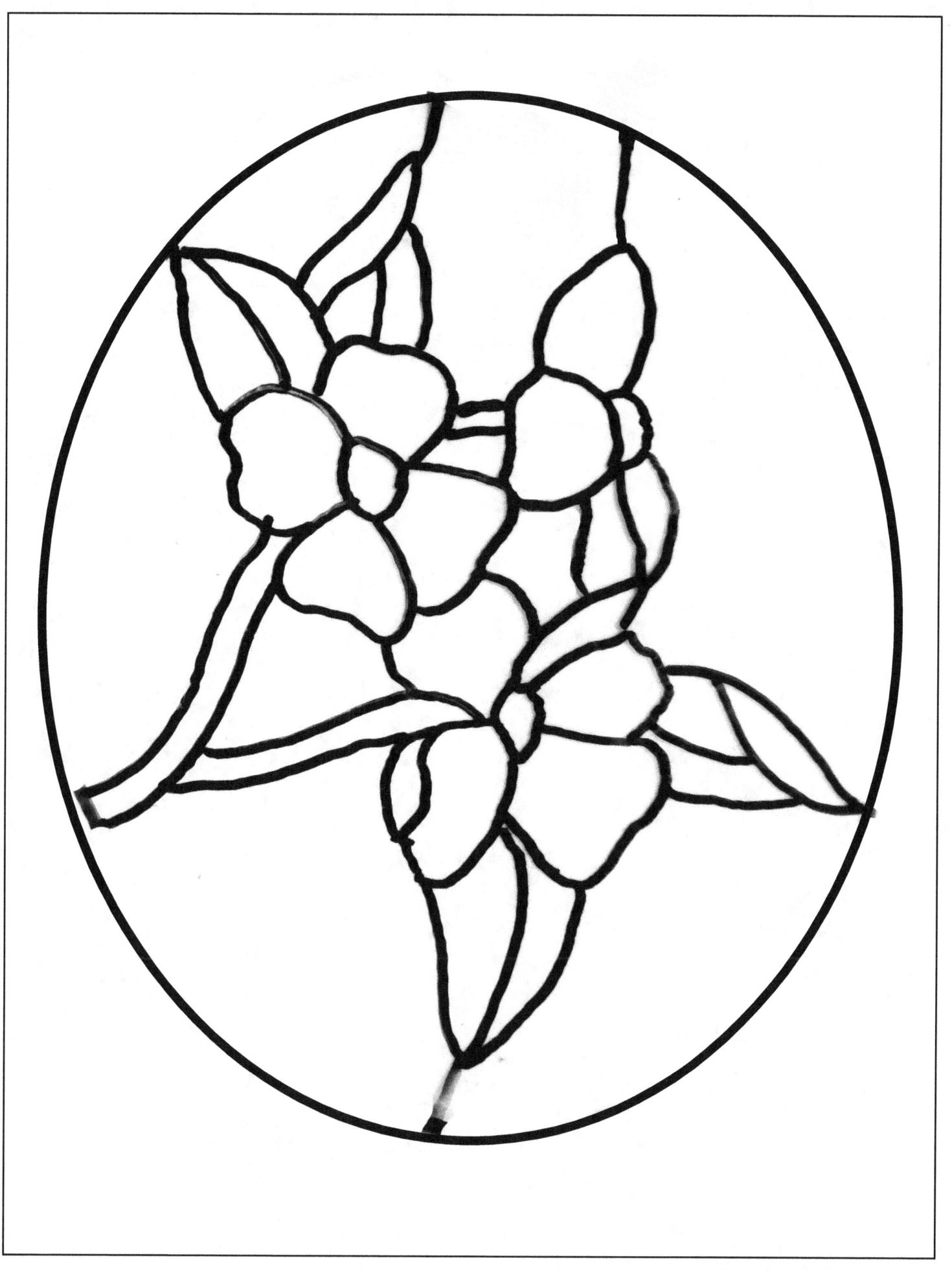

Brenda Schuls, *Magnolias*

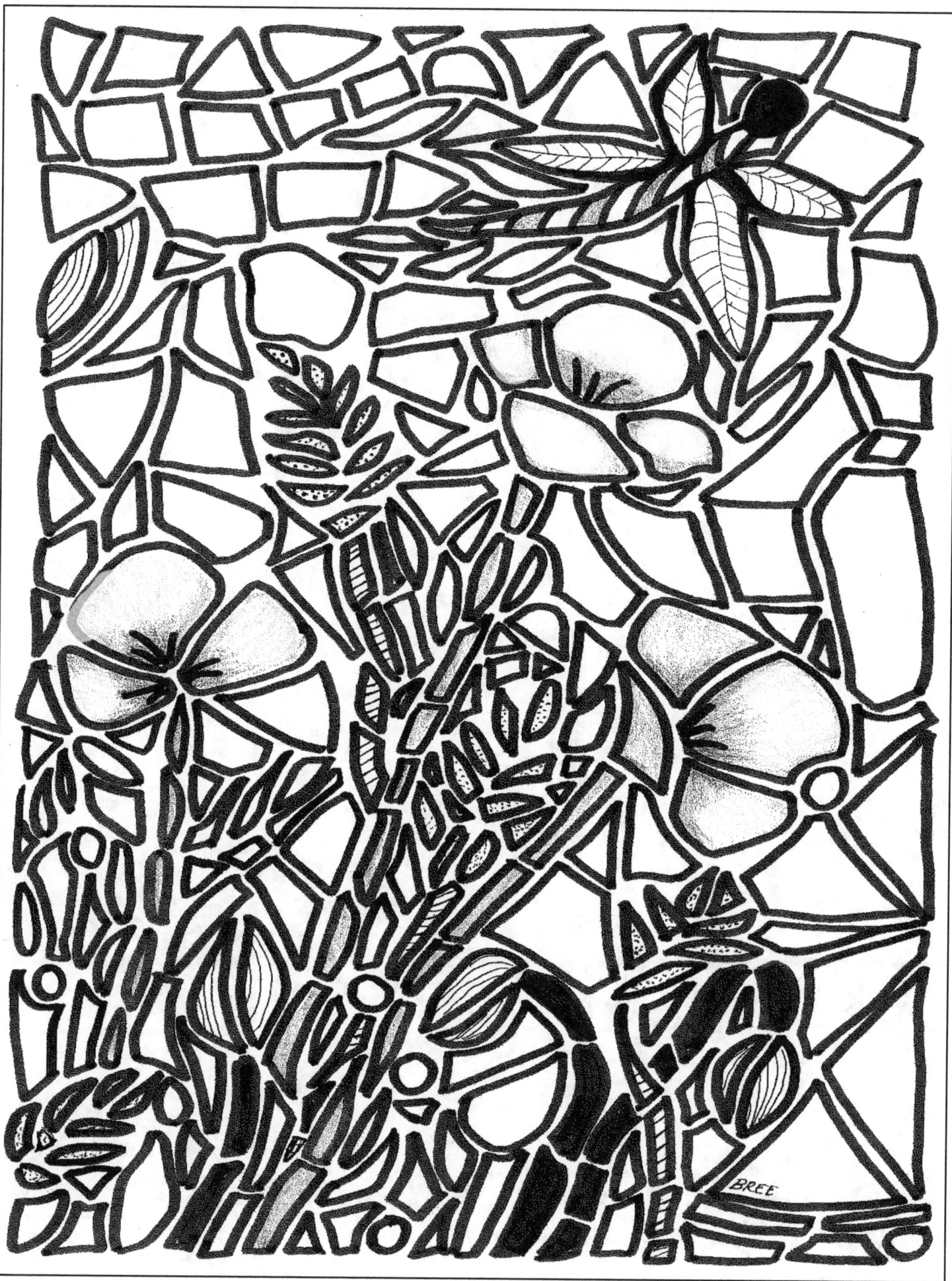

Brenda Thomas

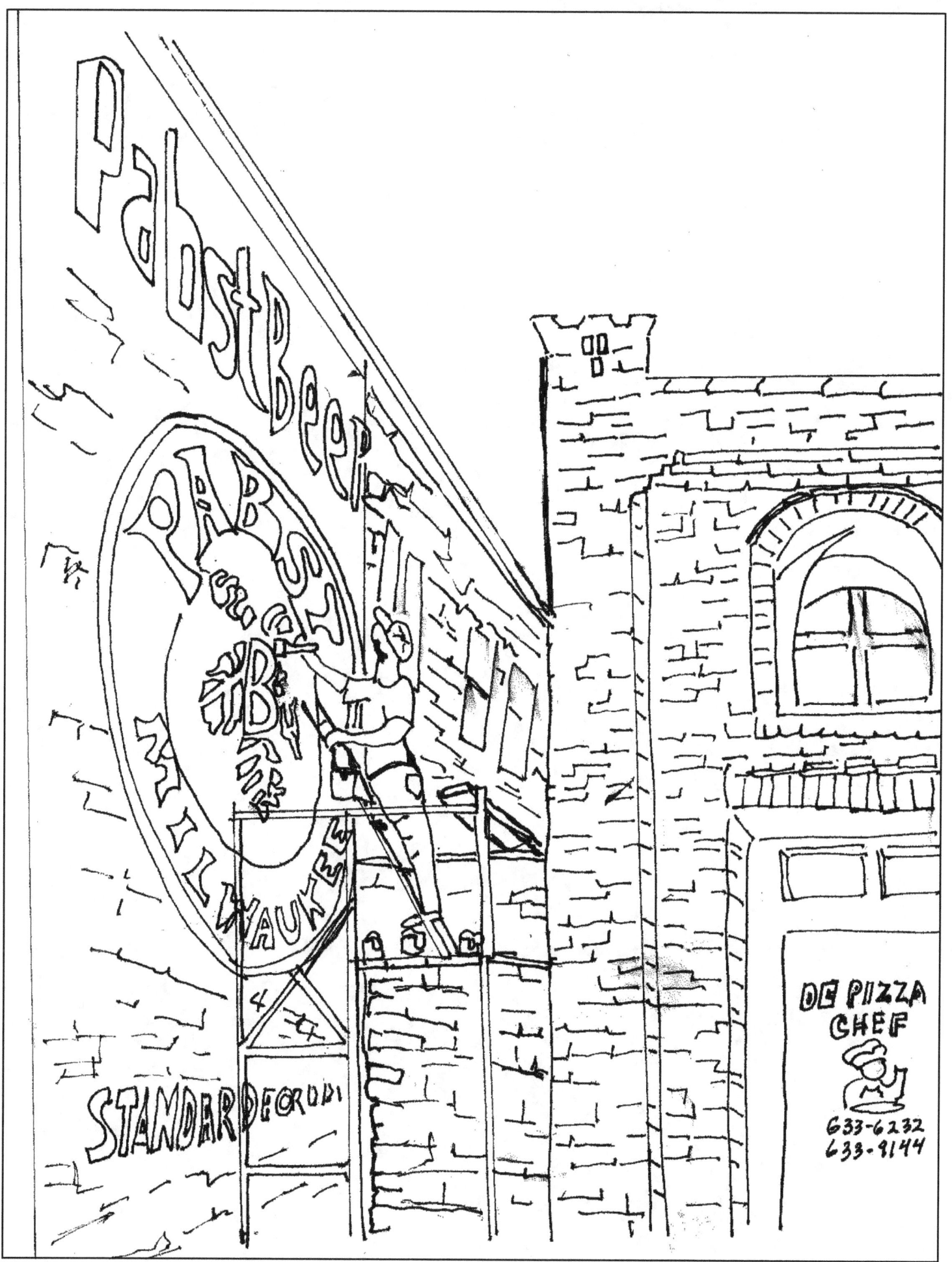

Caye Christensen, *Ivanhoe Pub and Grill*

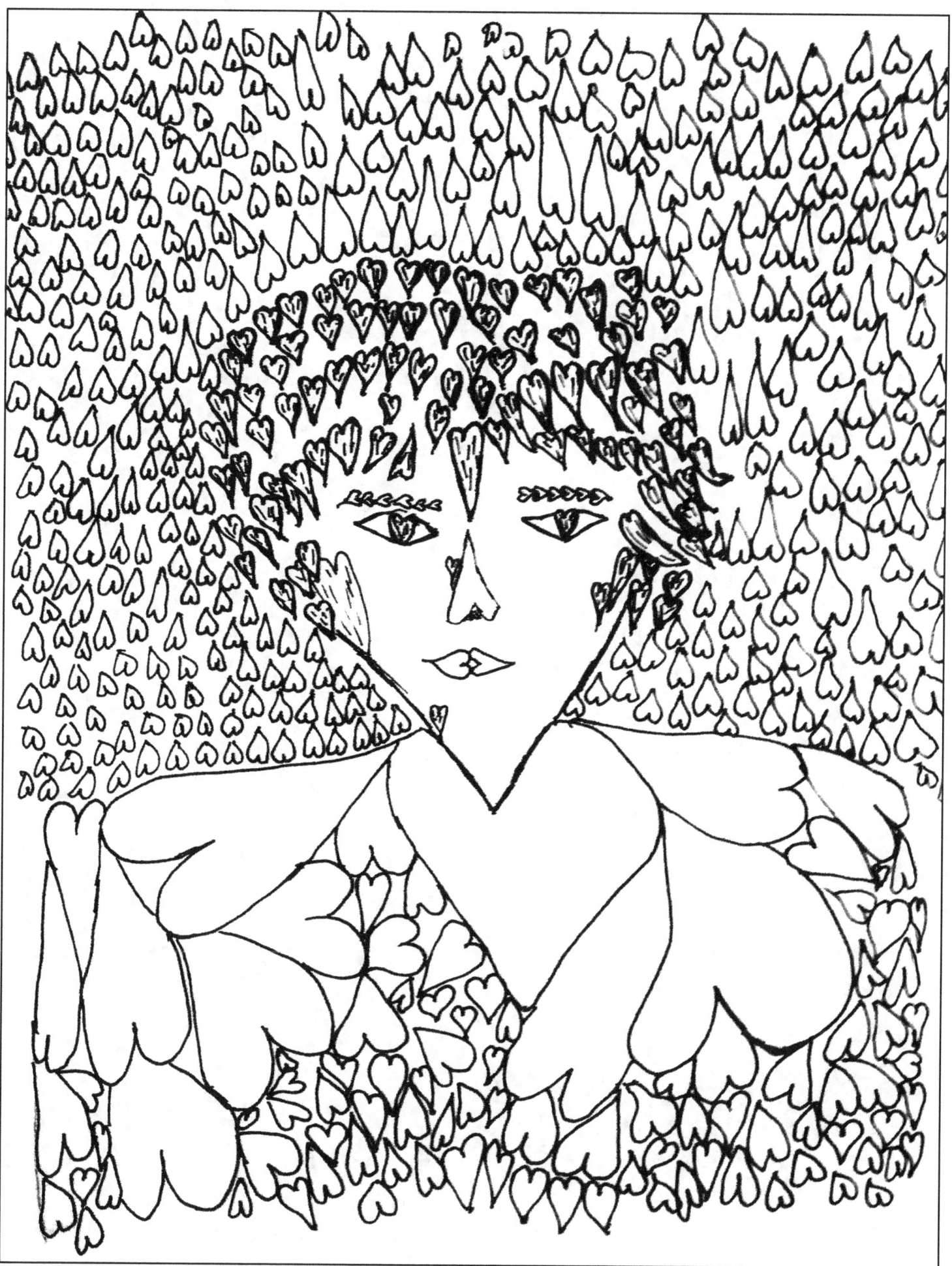

Cindy Bojcic, *Heart Art*

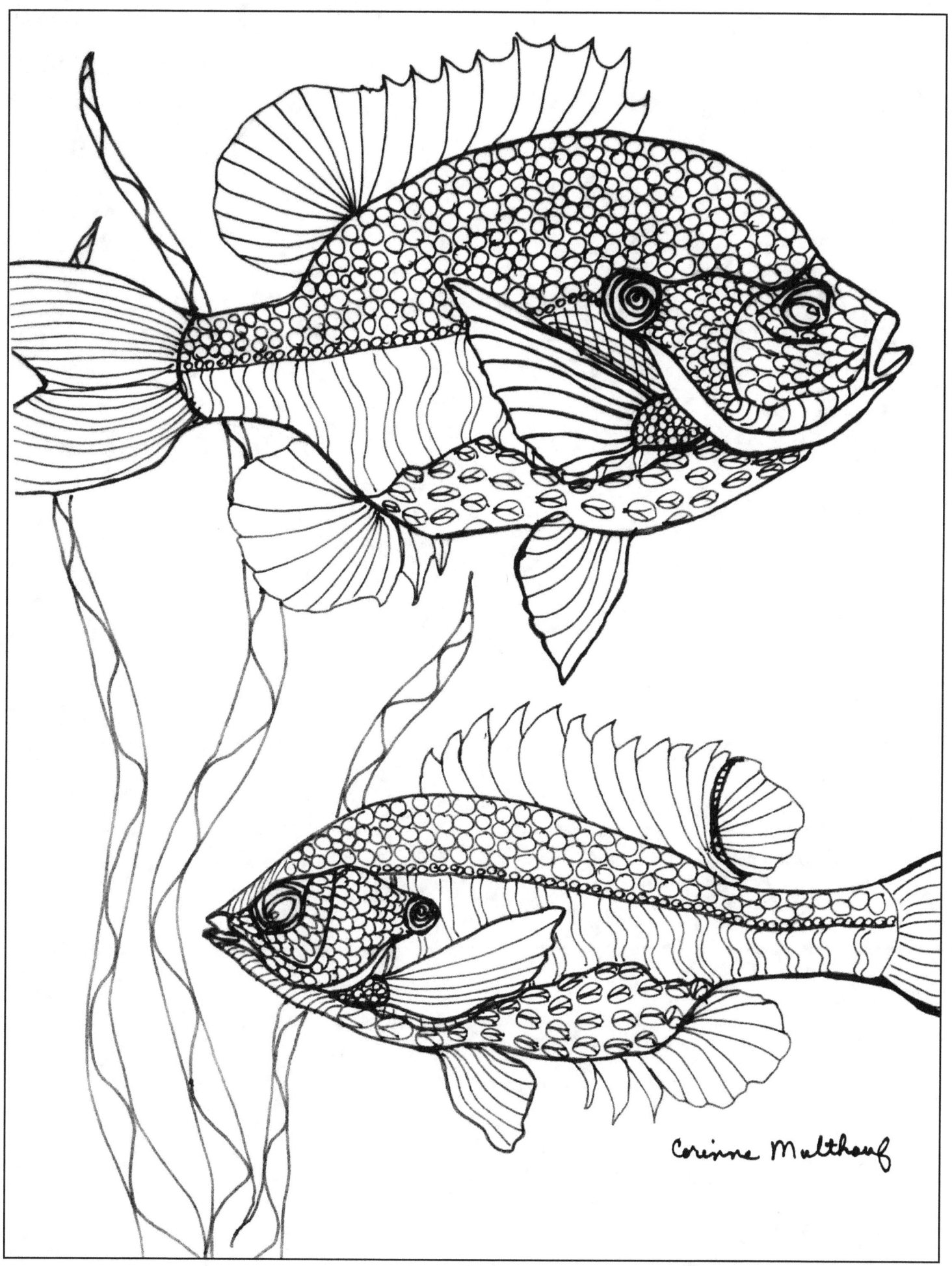

Corinne Multhauf, *Dreaming Bluegills*

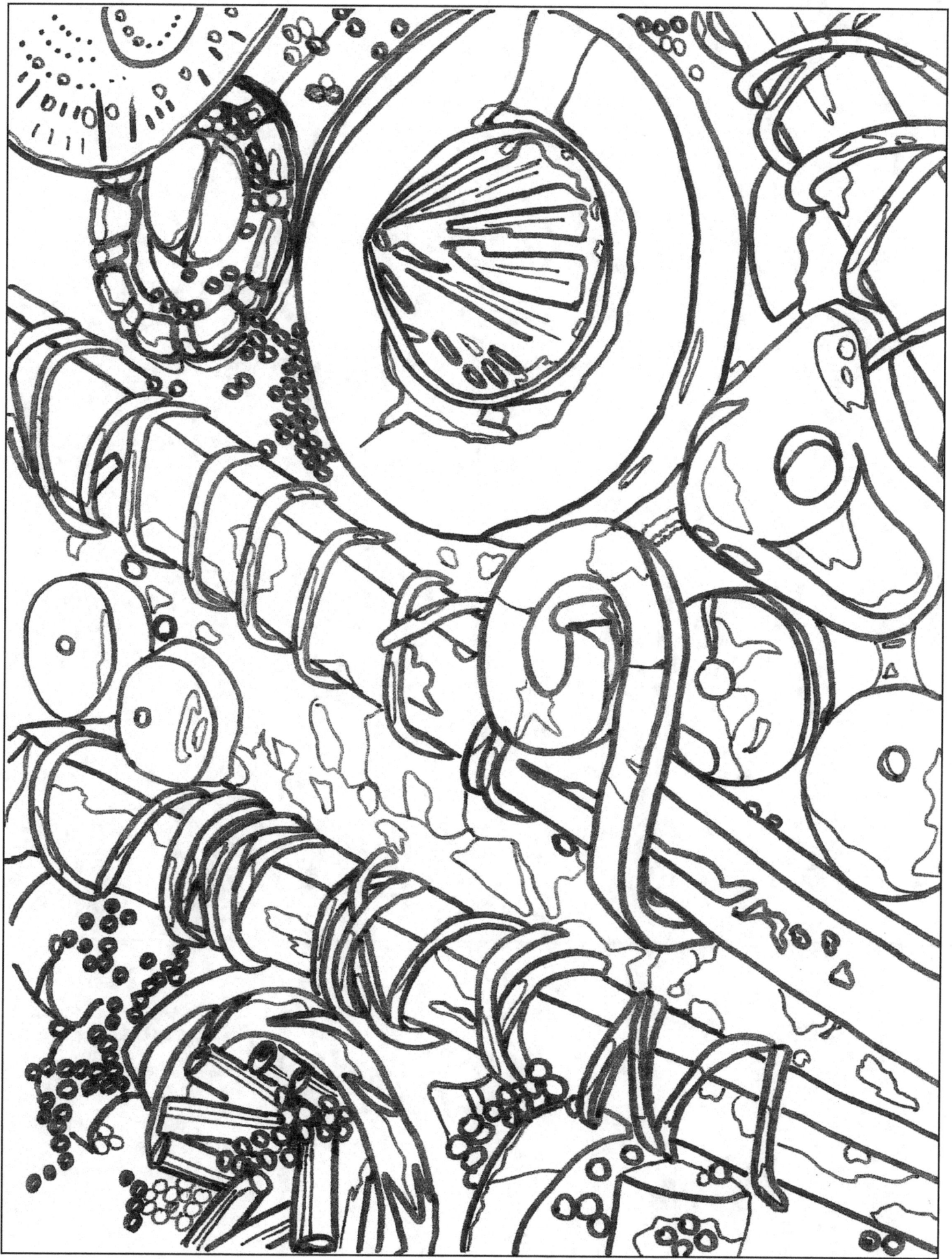

Tanja Martinez

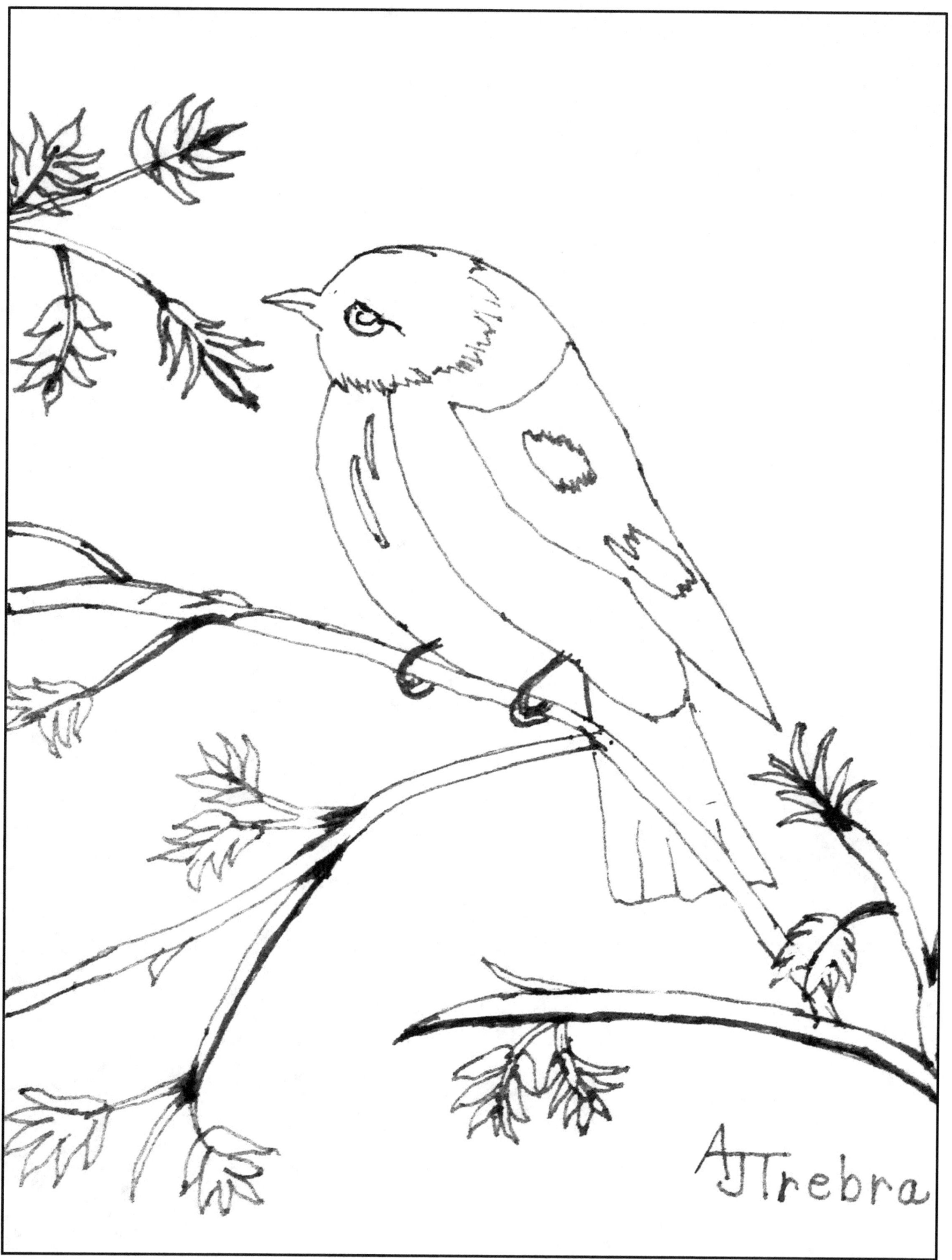

Ardath Trebra, *Western Tanager*

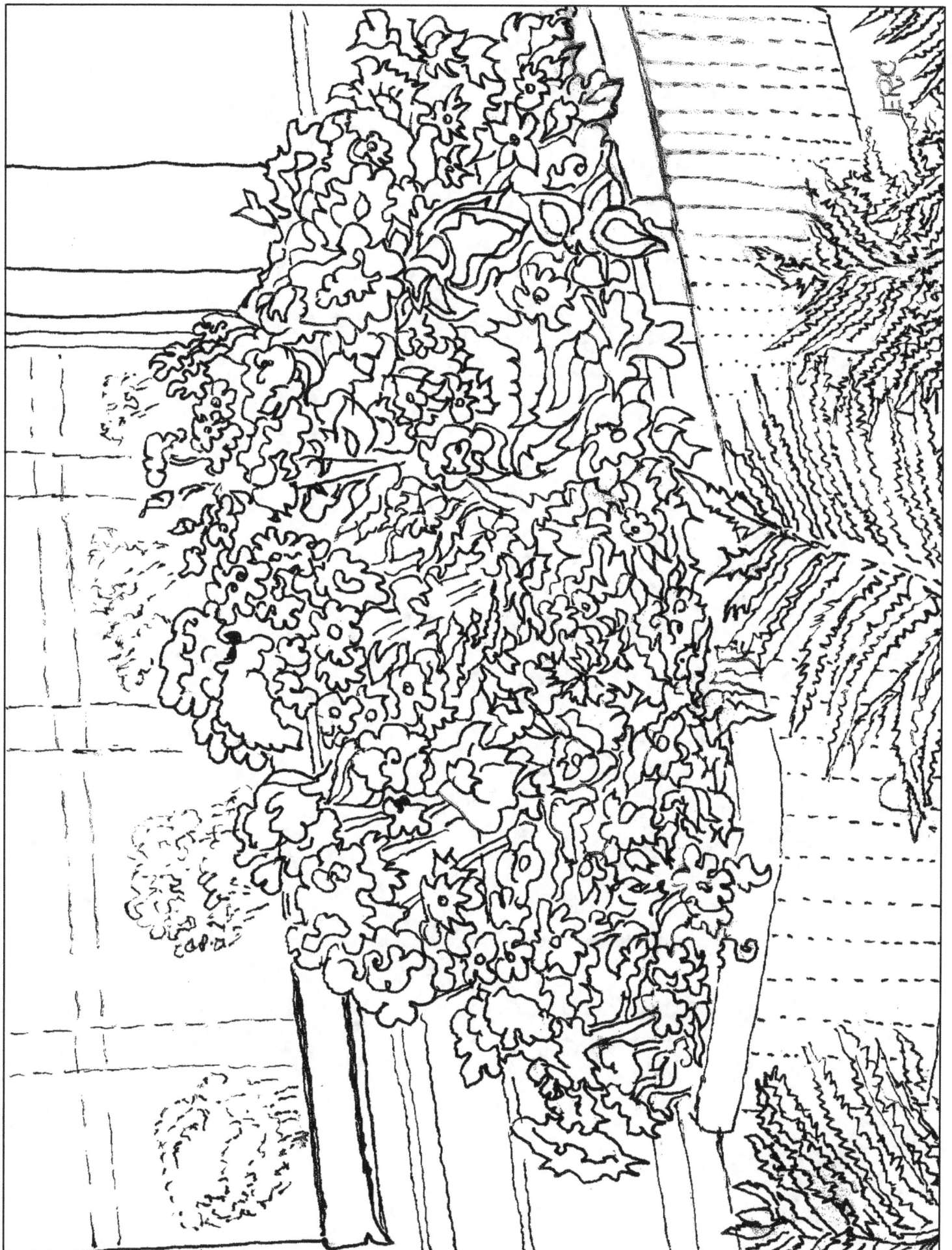

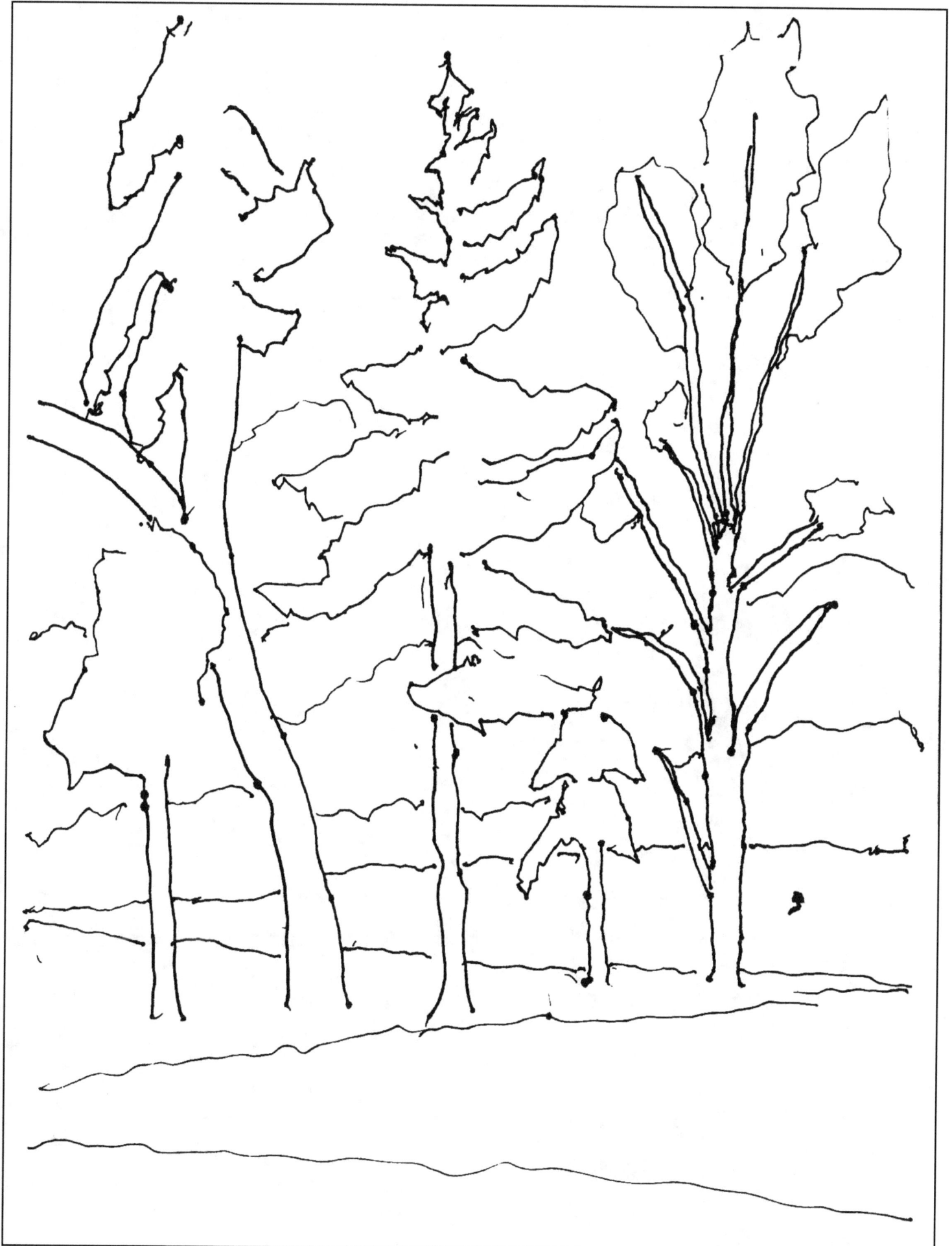

Jane Hamlin

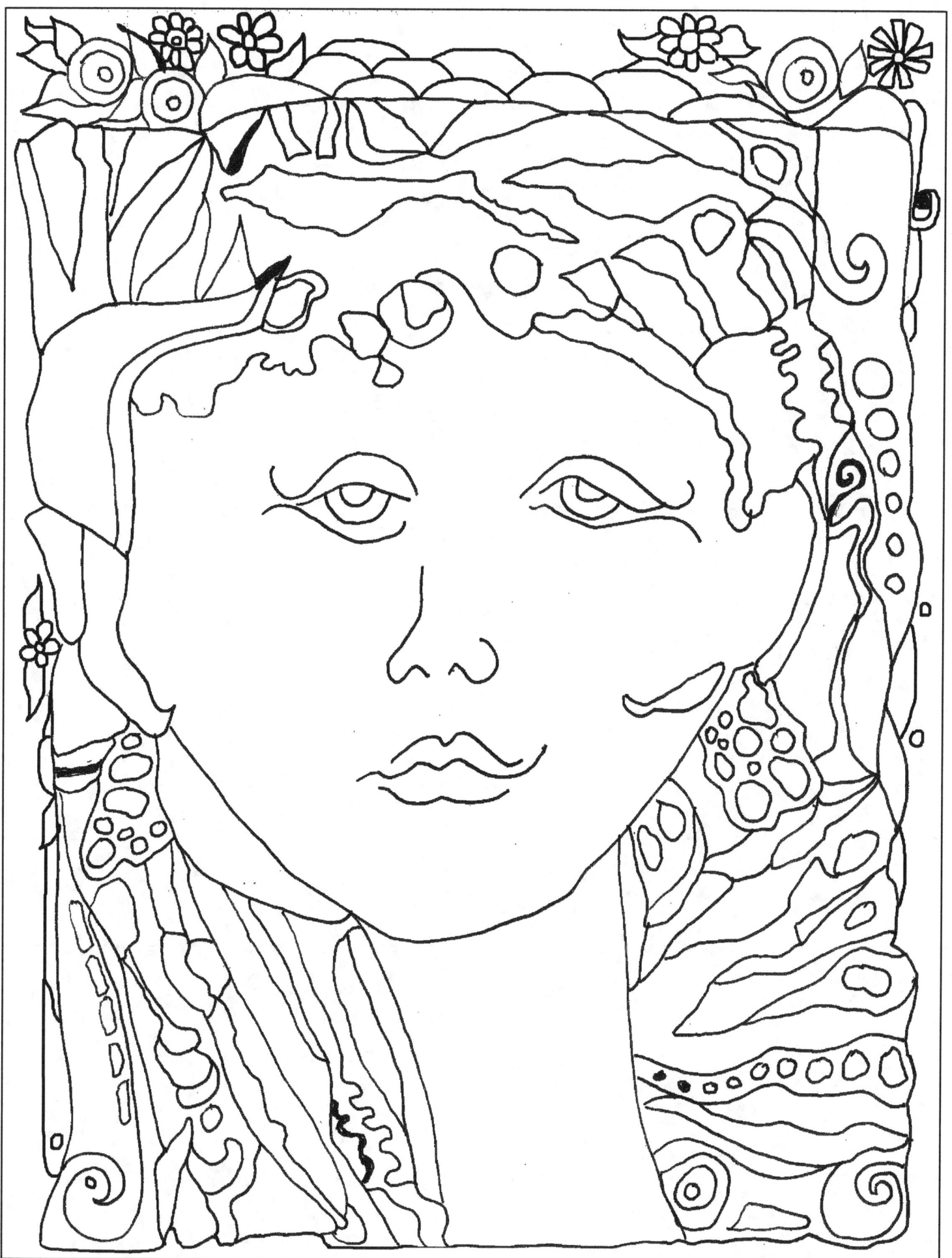

Janet Mrazek, *Portrait Collage*

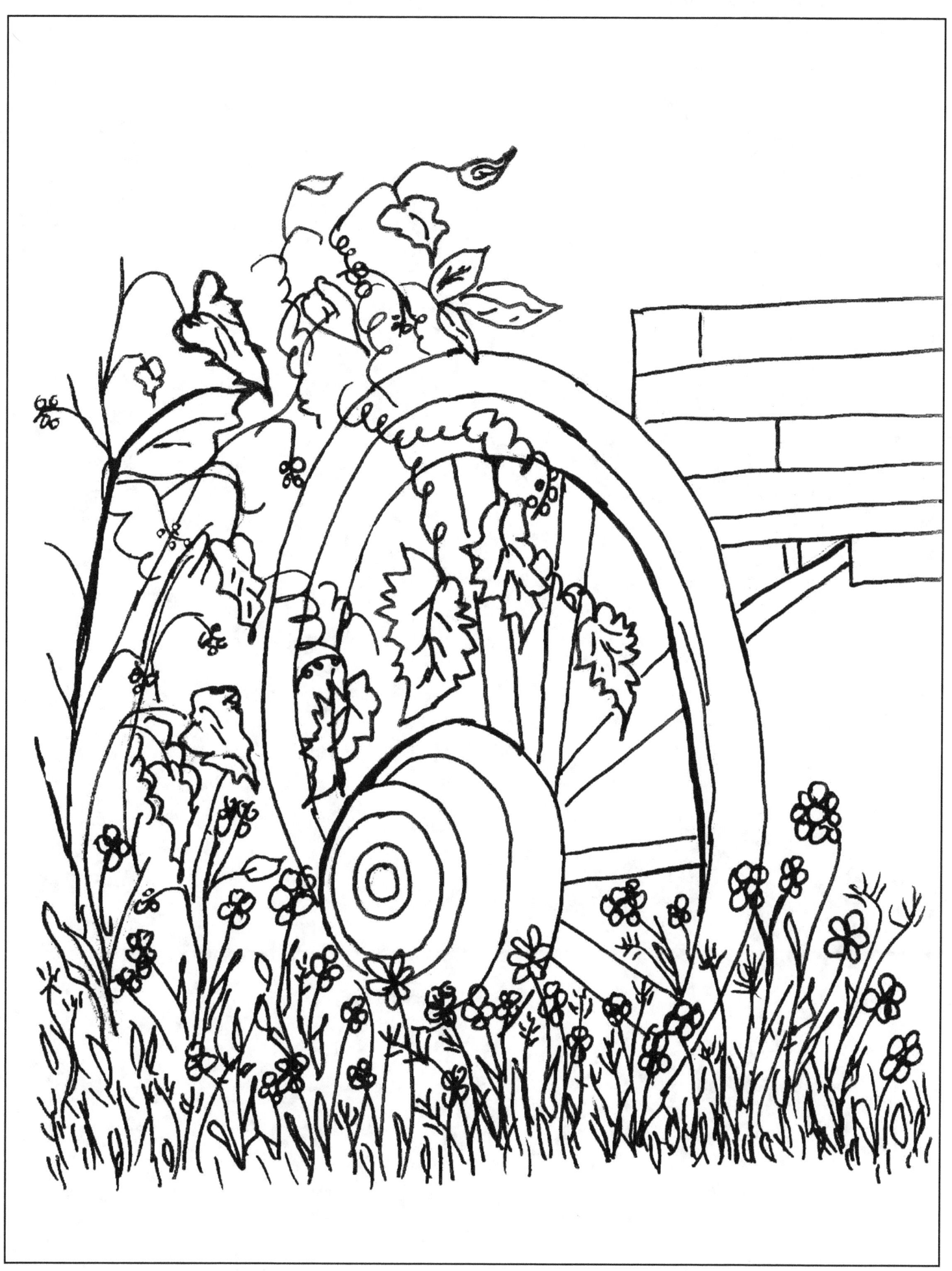

Jill Castillo, *Wagon Wheel Garden*

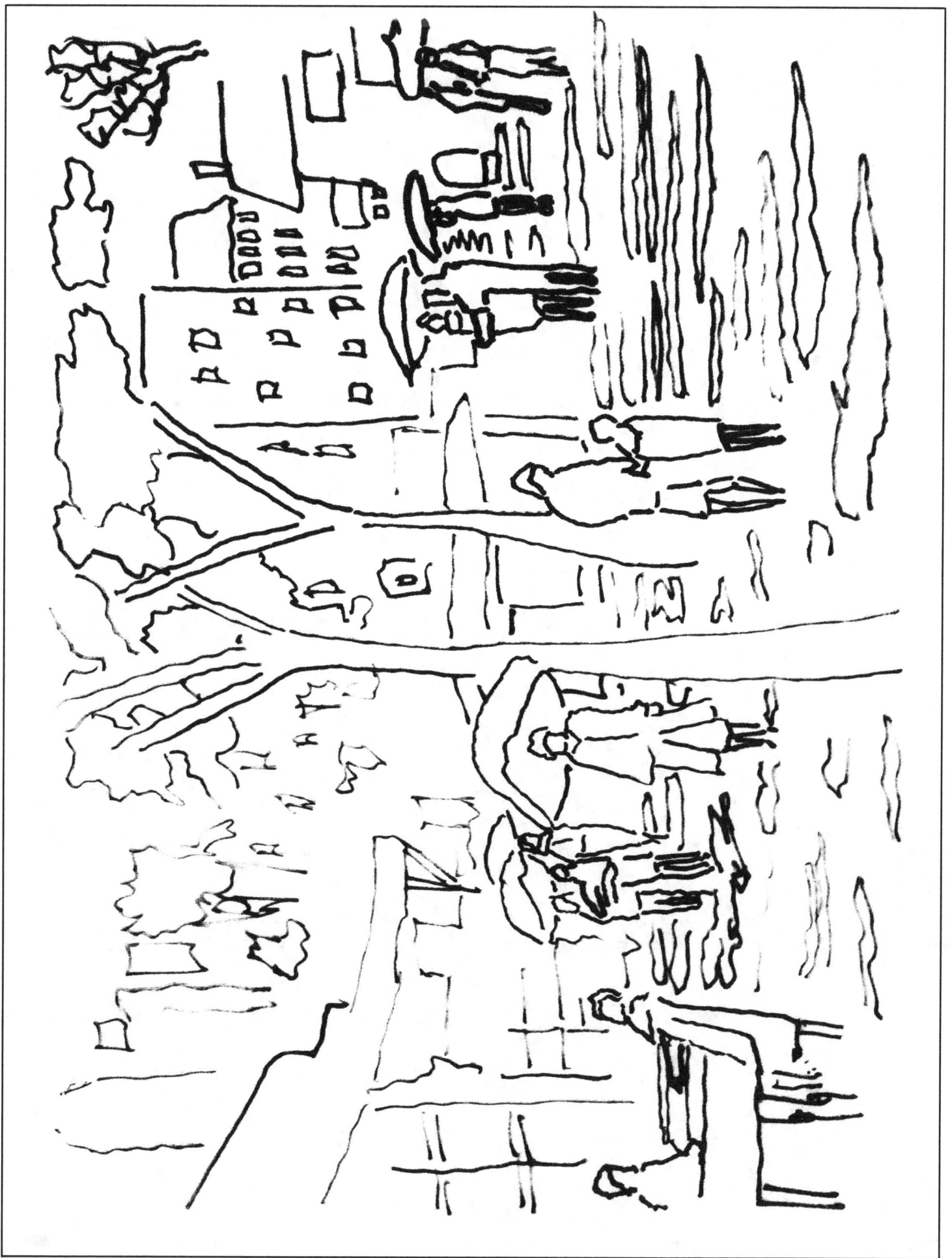

Joe Van Hulle, *Paris in the Rain*

31

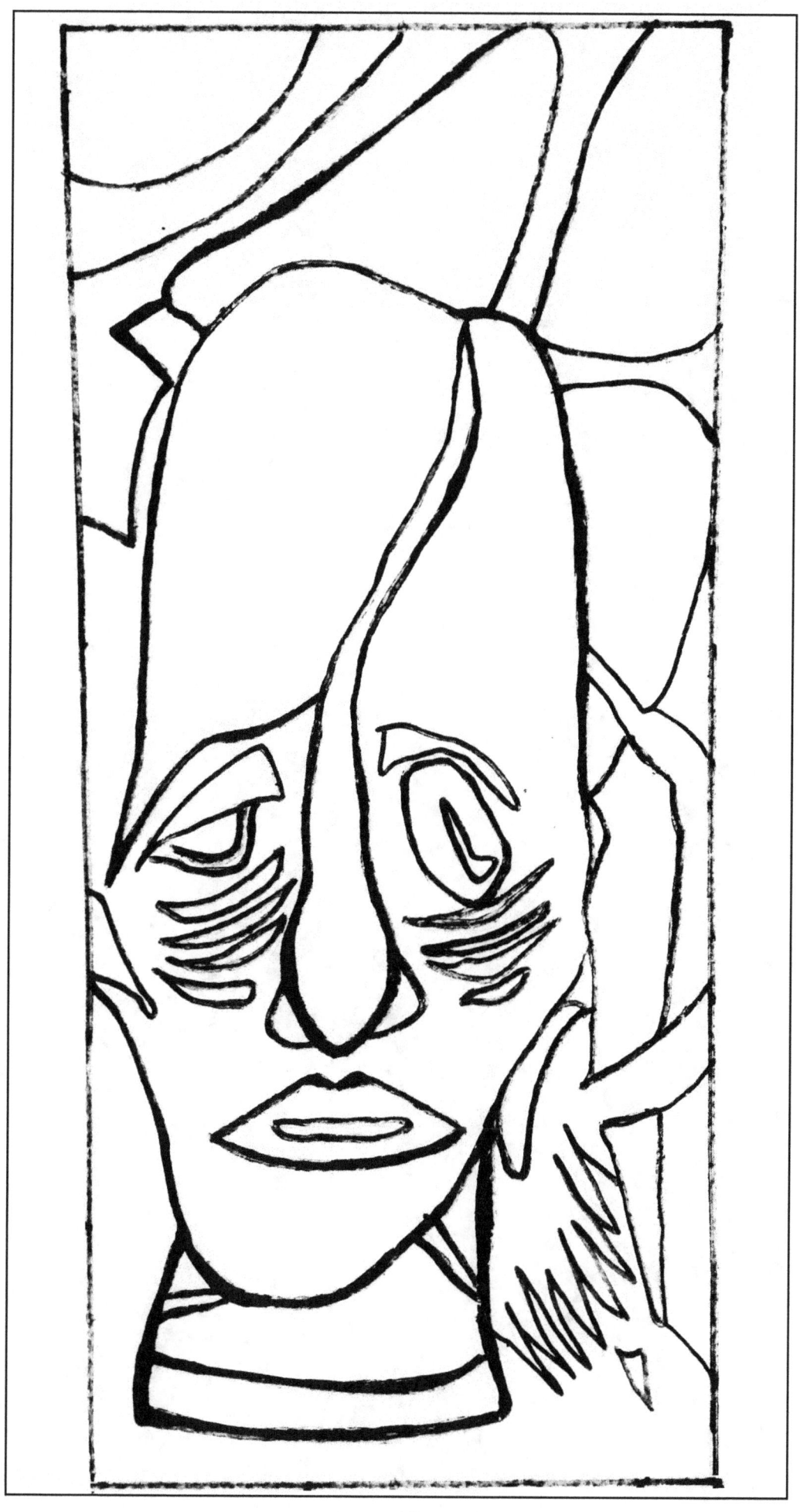

33

Julie Peterson

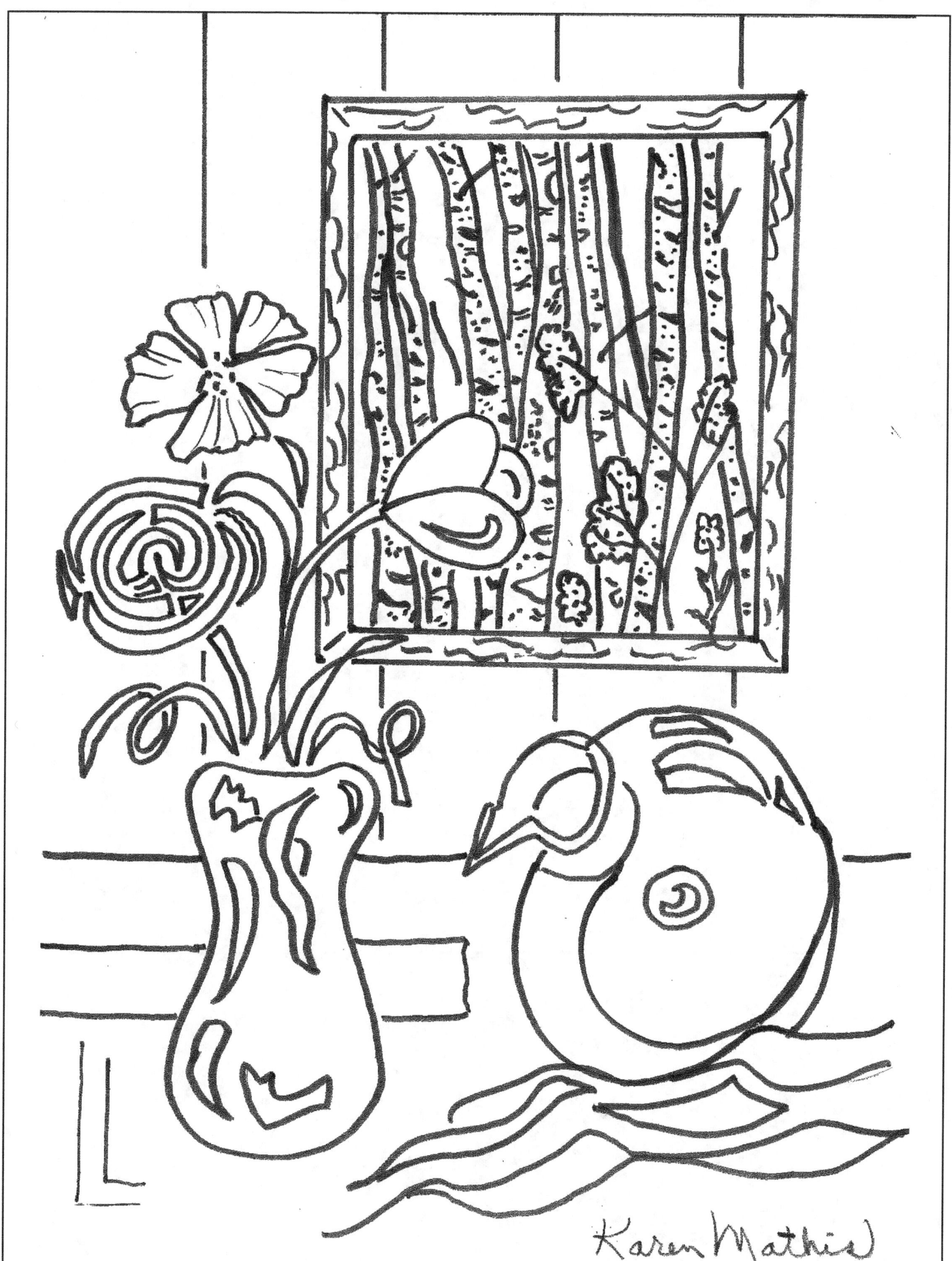

Karen Mathis, *Still Life*

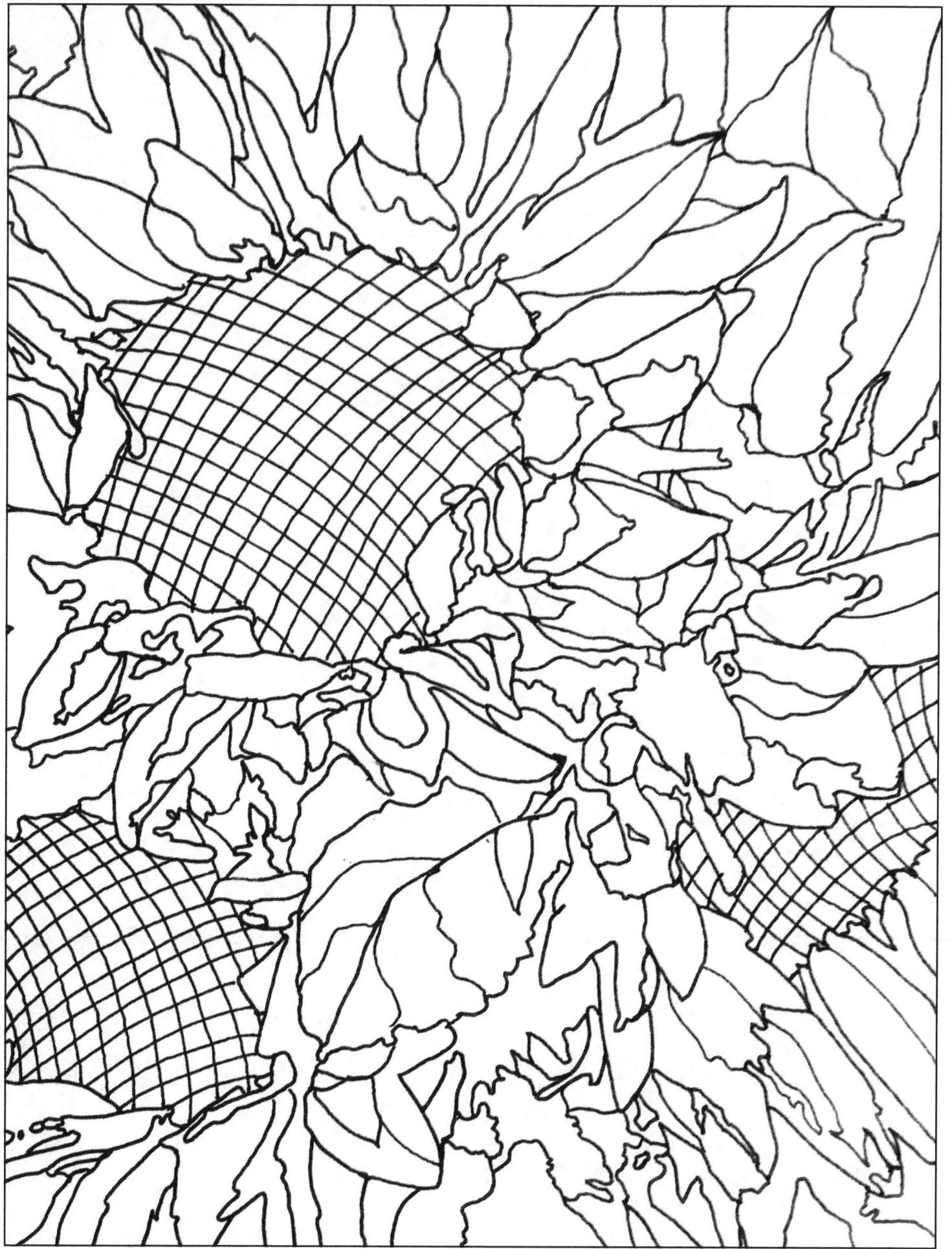

Kate Peterson, *Sunflowers*

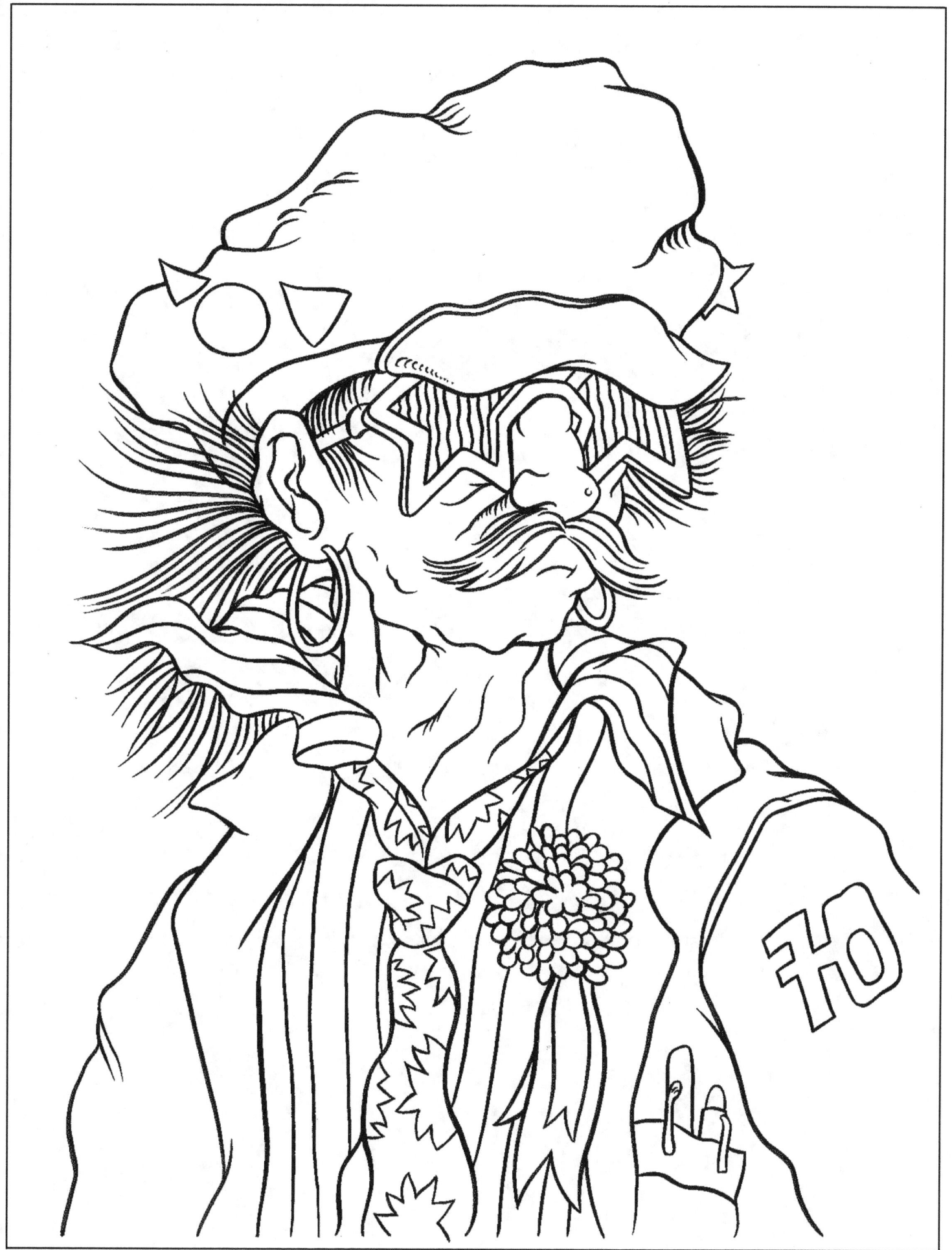

Lance Raichert

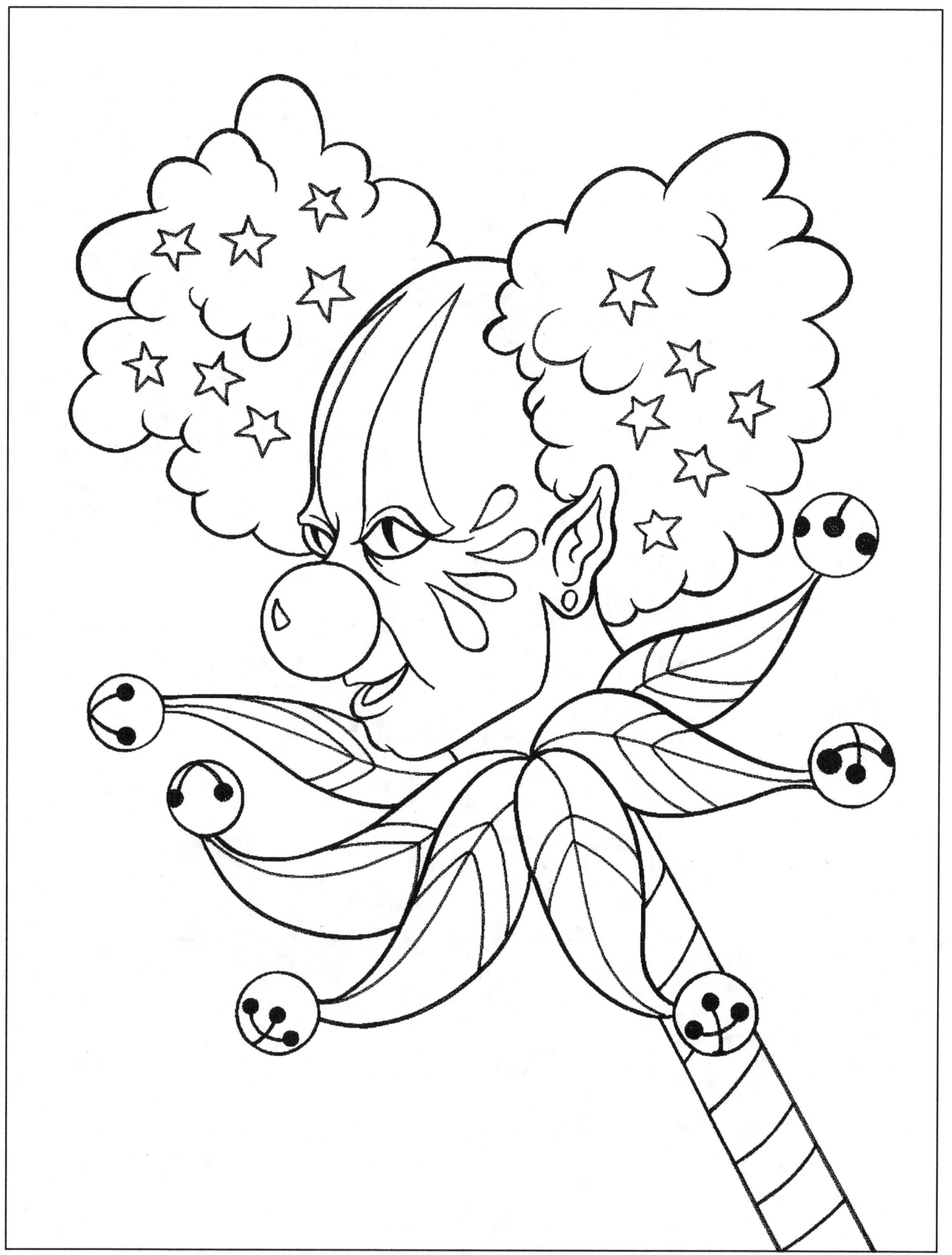

Lance Raichert

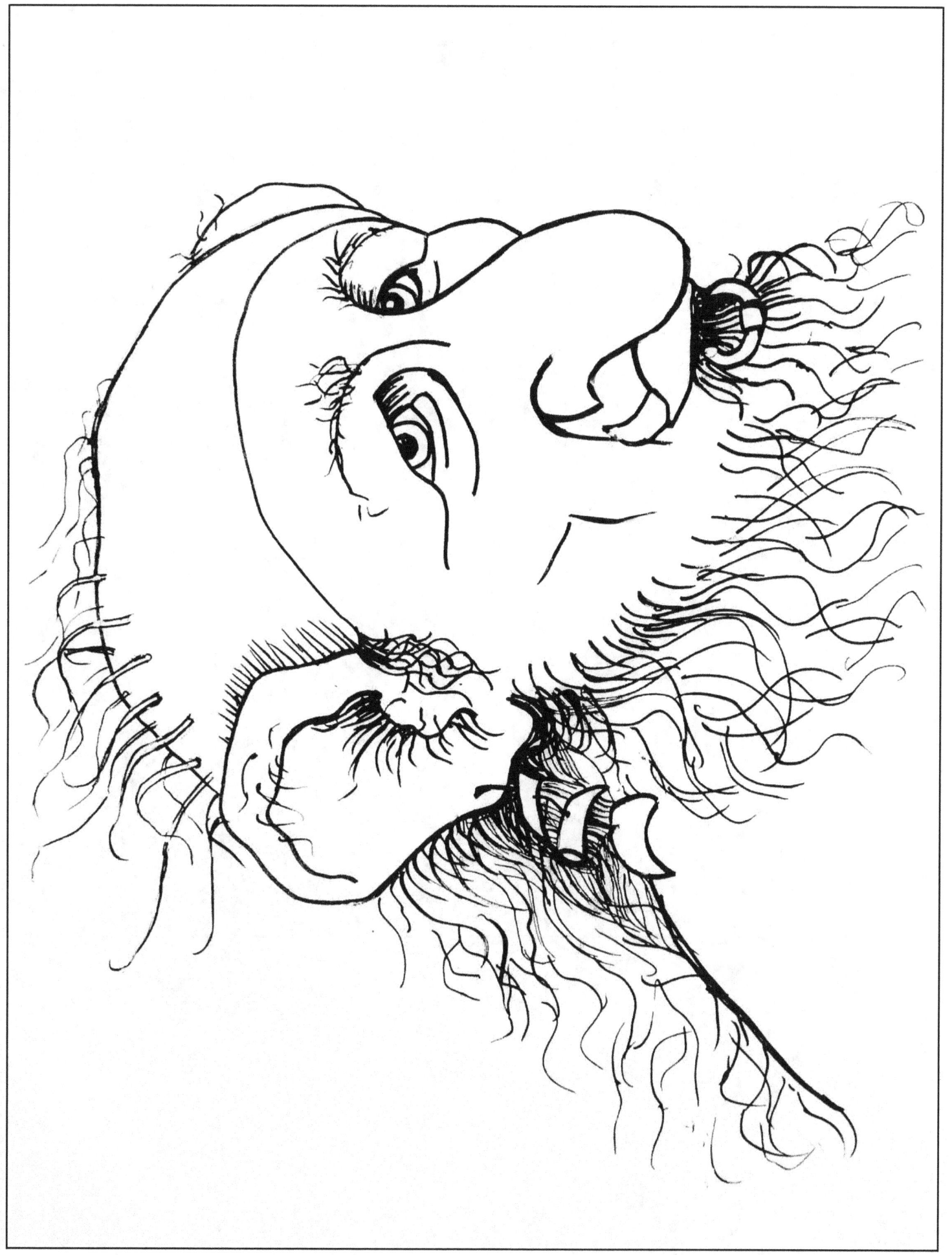

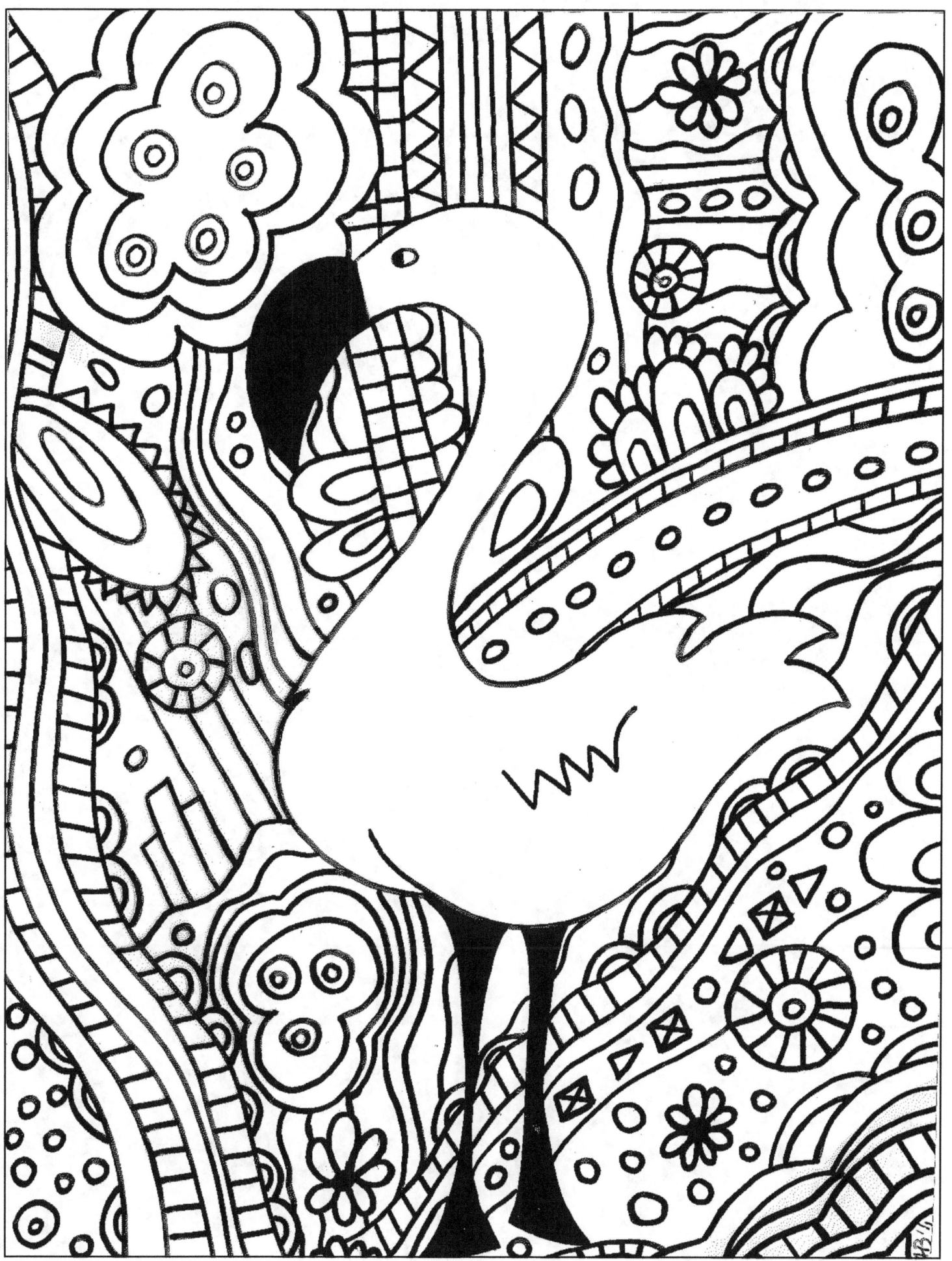

Mary Ann Bresnahan, *Flamingo Schmingo*

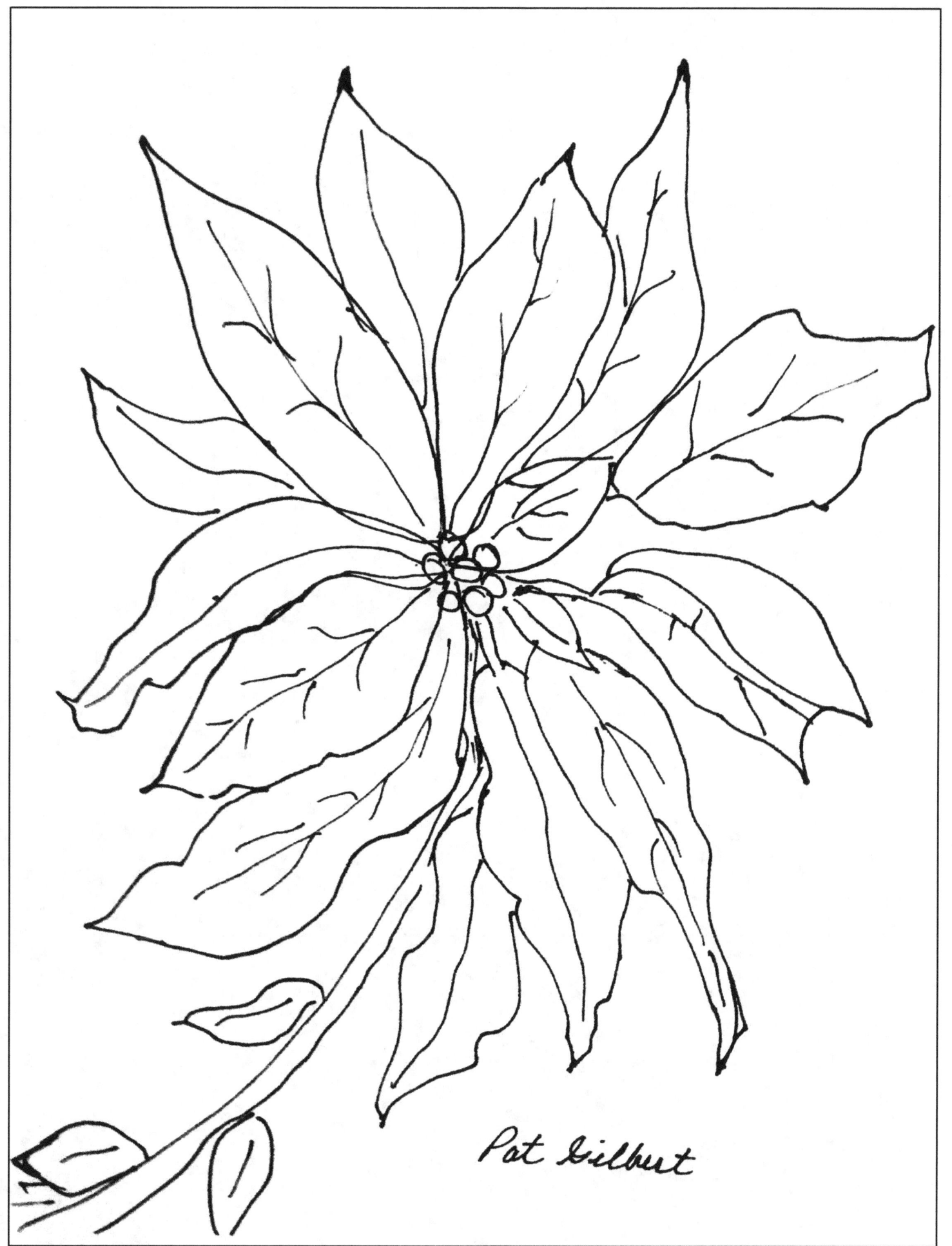

Pat Gilbert

Pat Gilbert

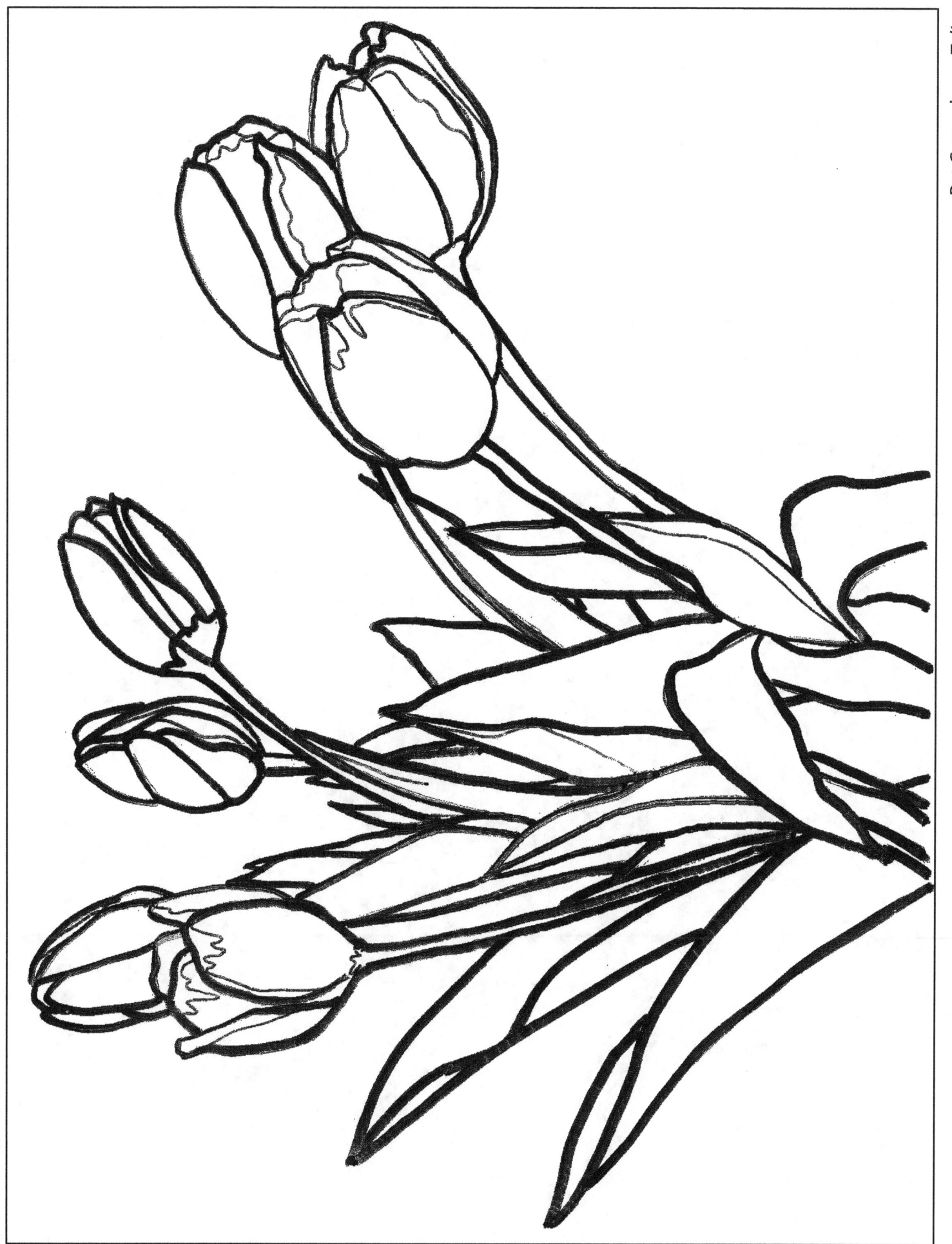

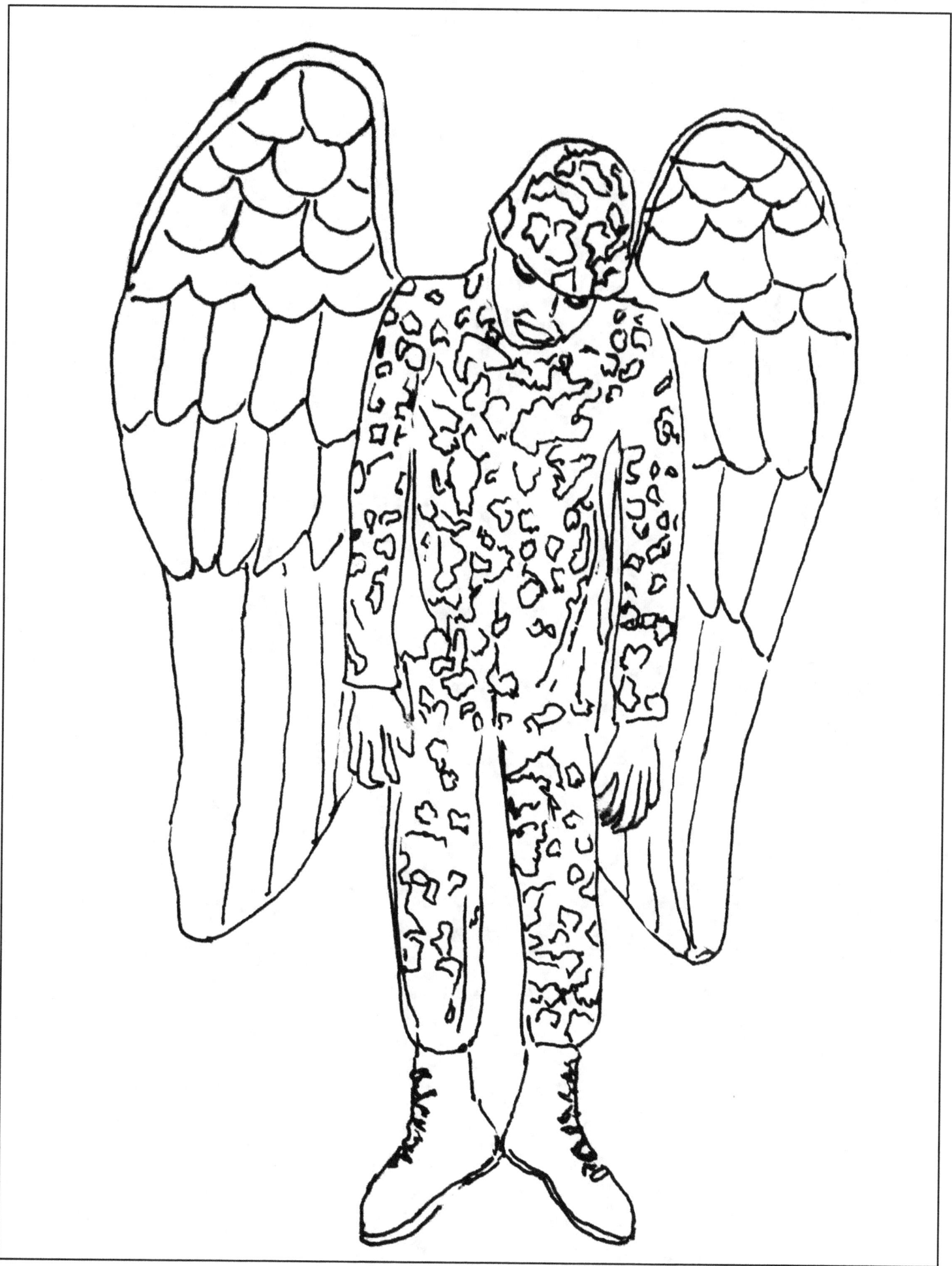

Russ Bohn

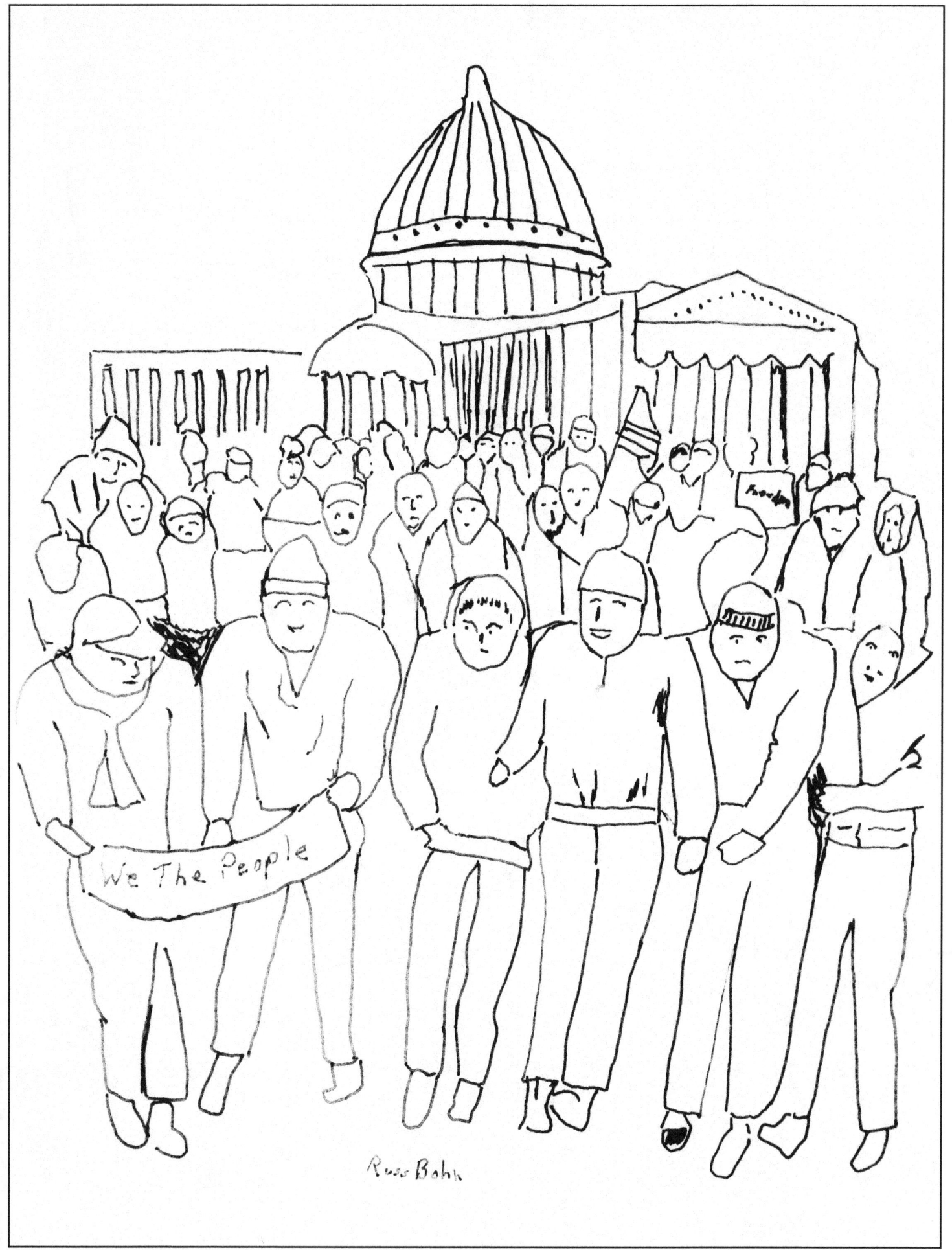

53

Russ Bohn, *We the People*

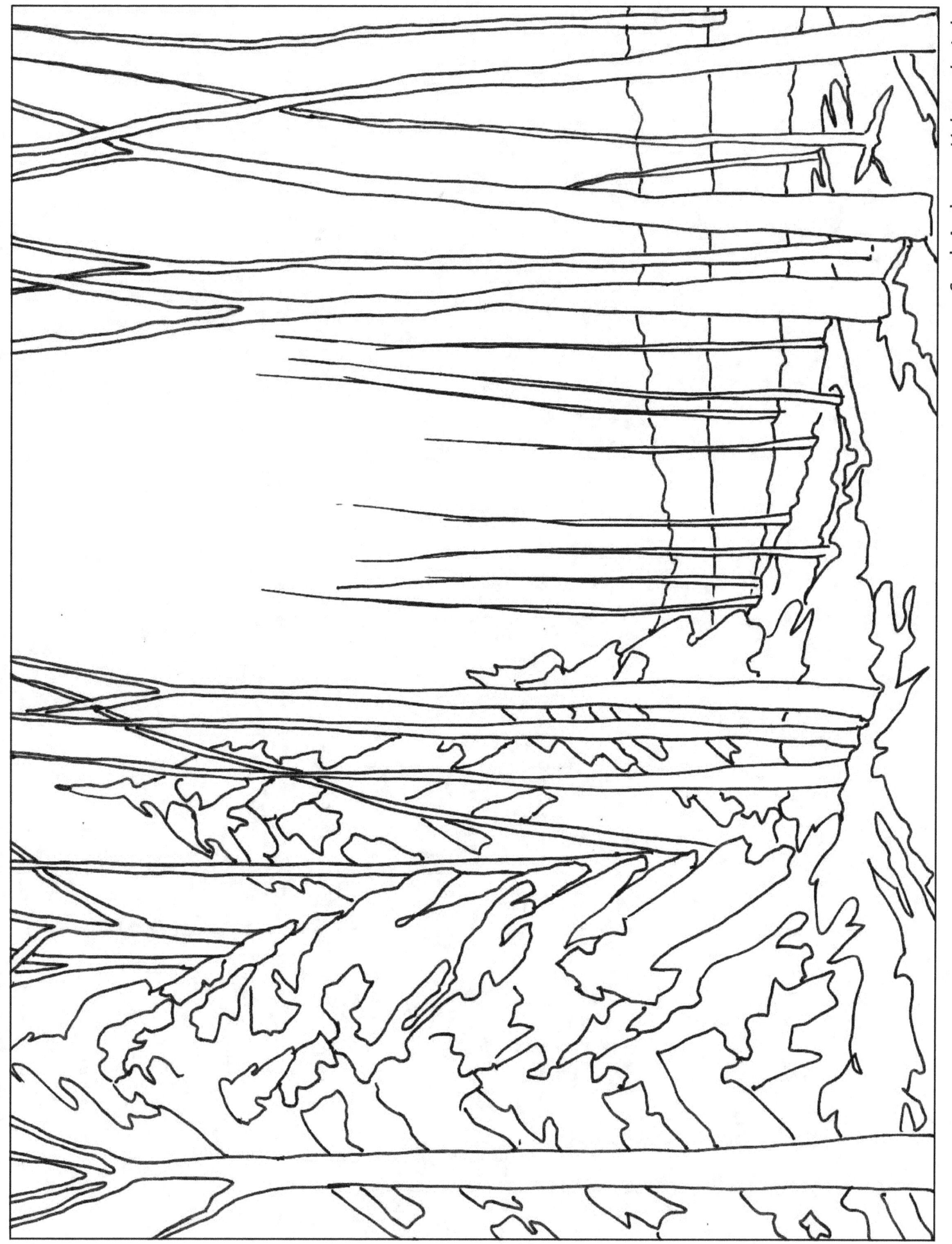

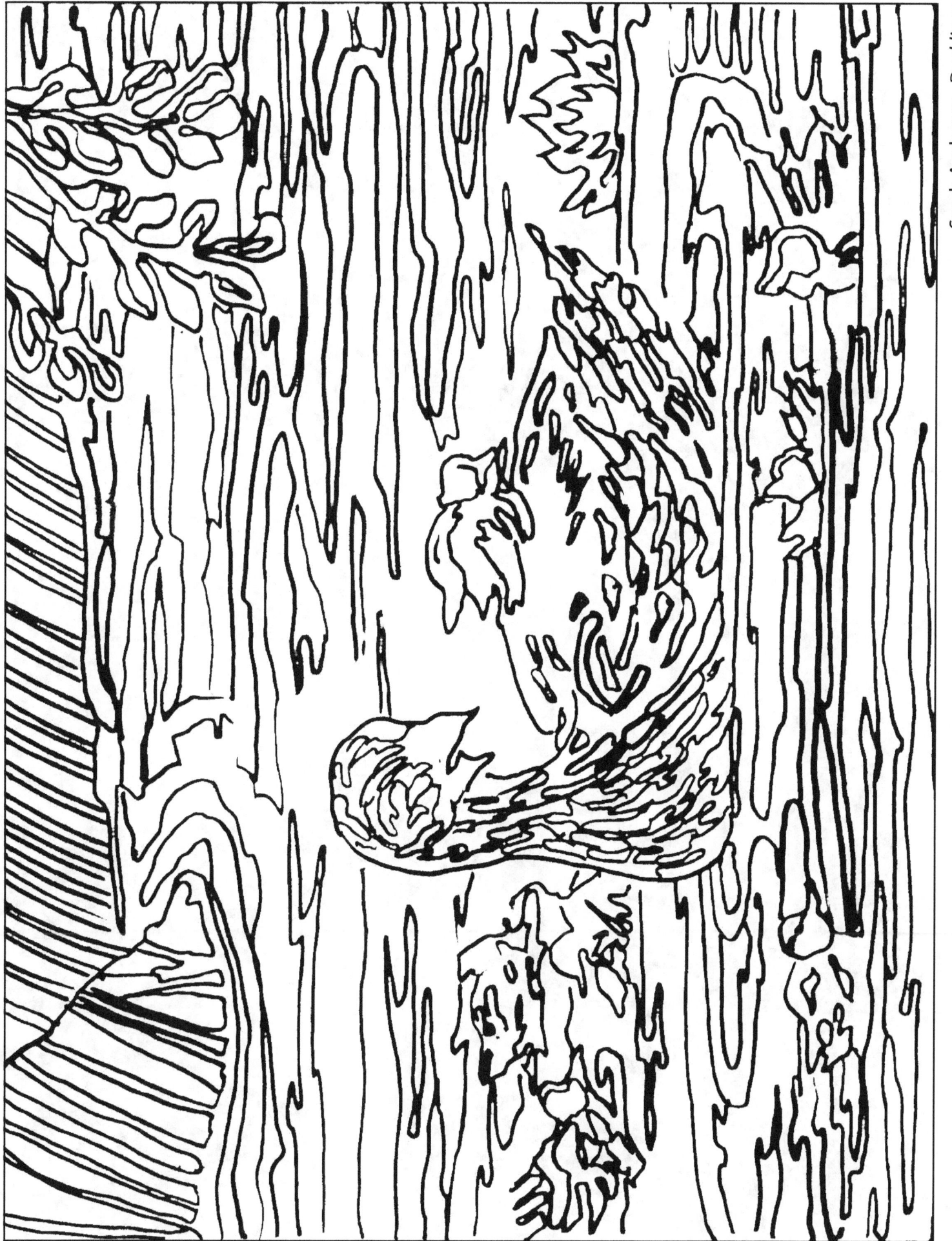

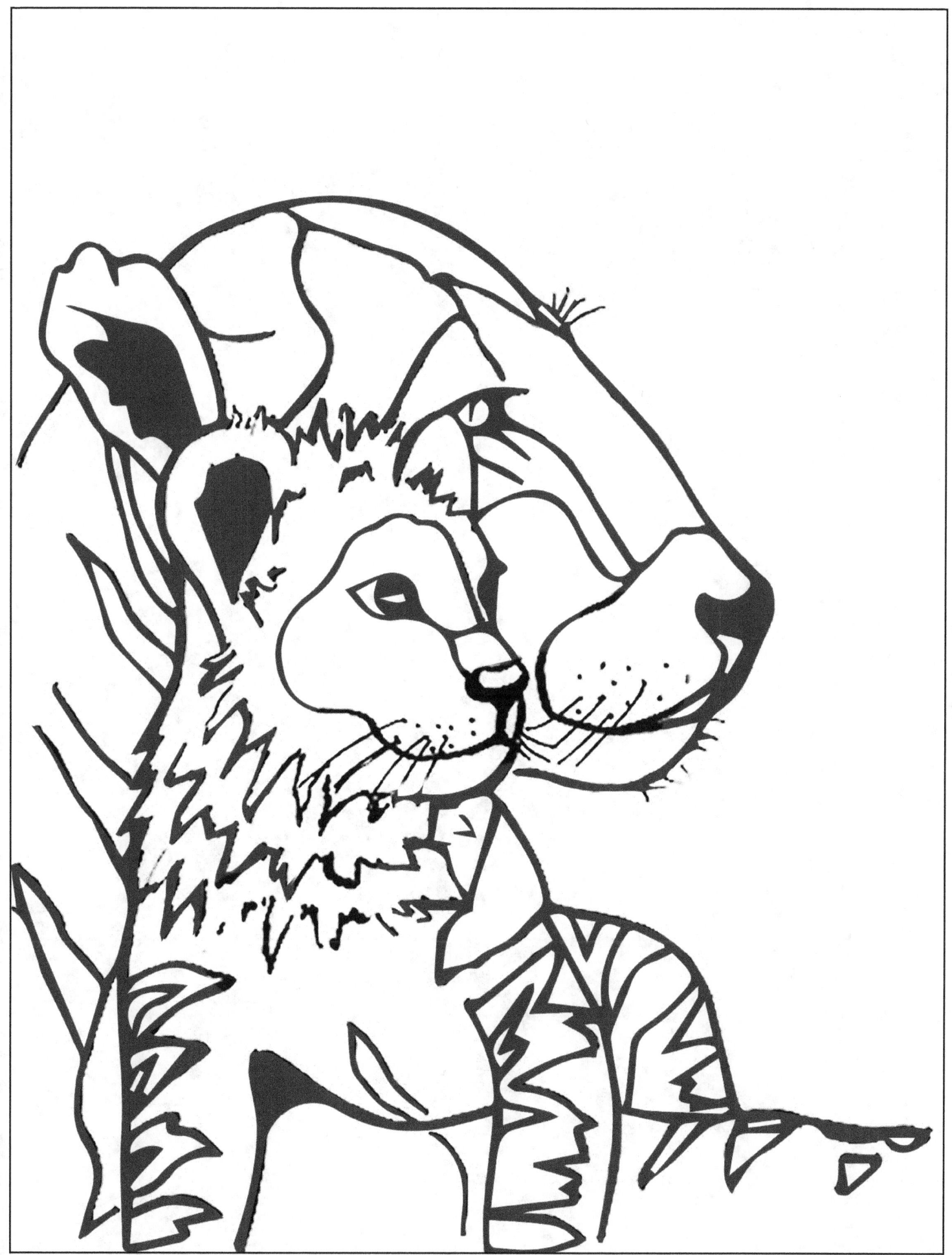

Sue Horton, *Protected*

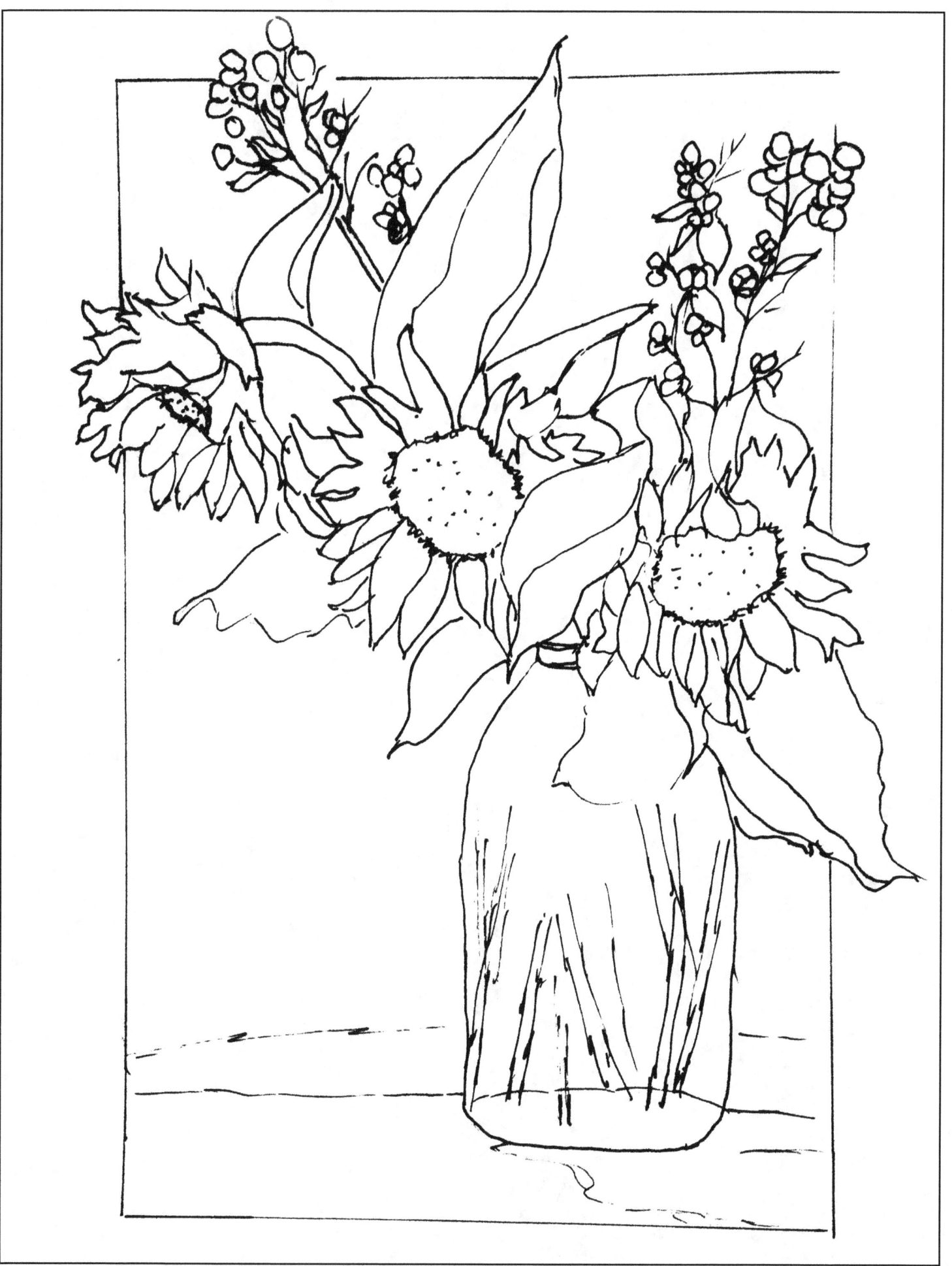

Suzanne Schackelman, *Praying Ladies*

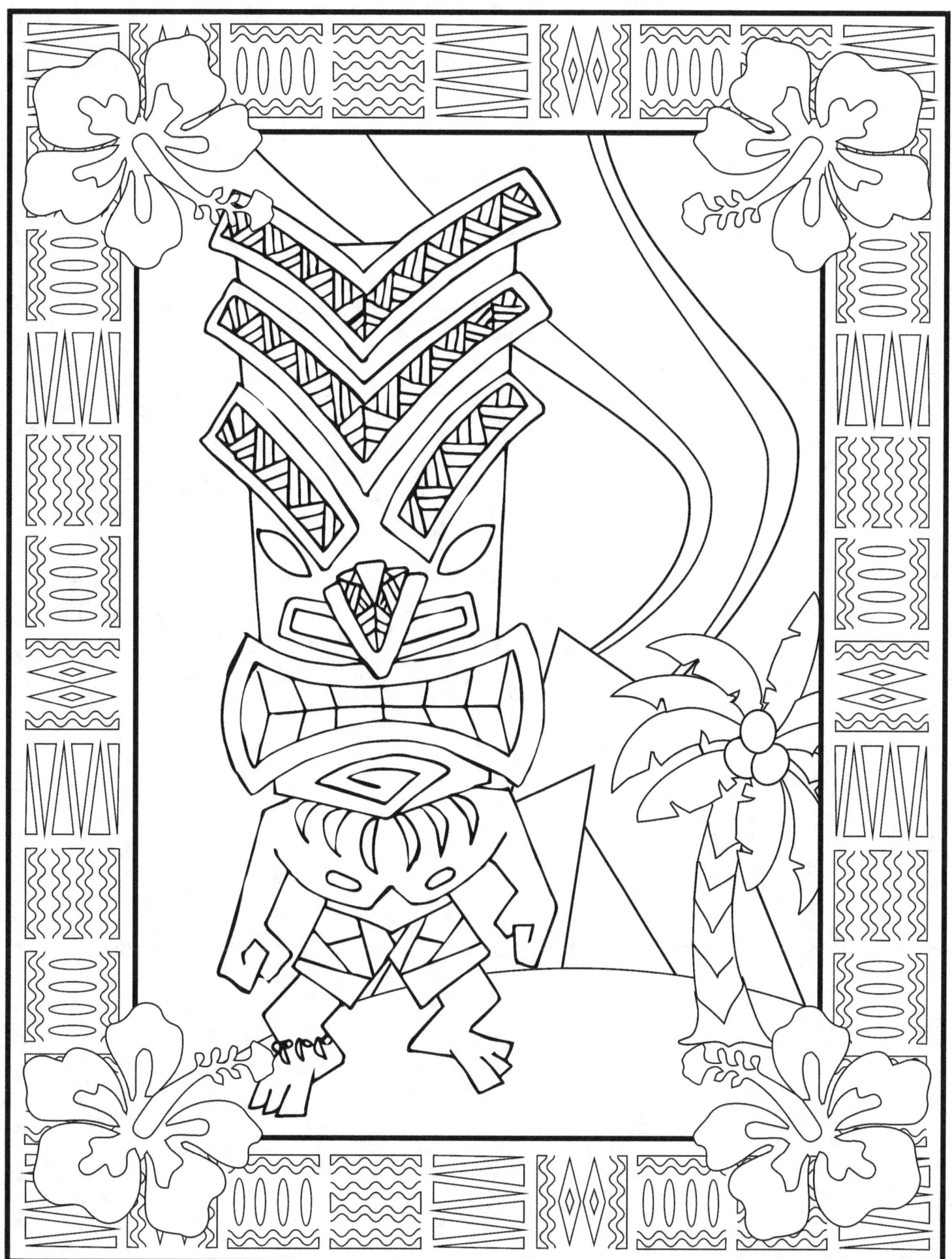

Wes Fallon, *Nui Tiki Island*

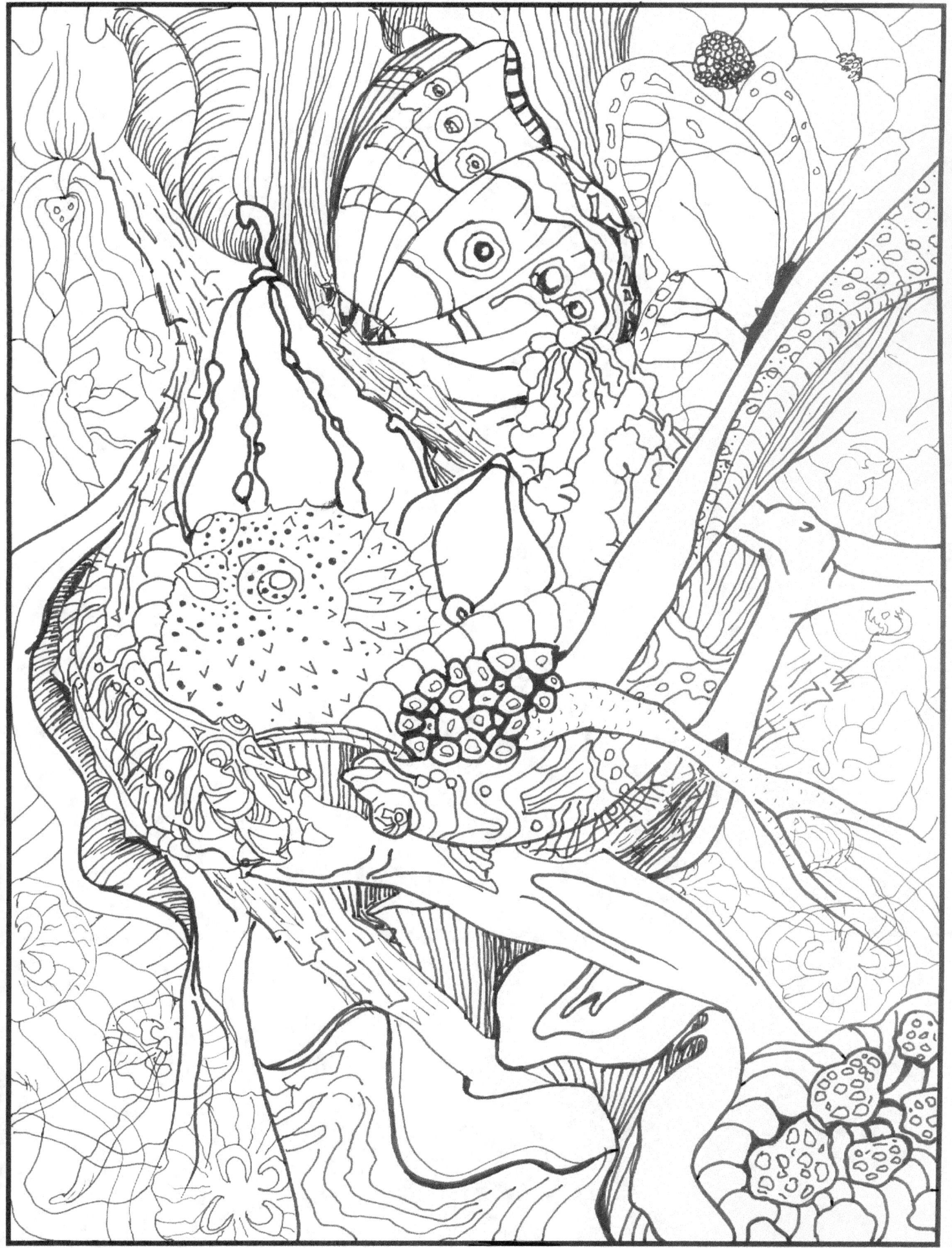

Patricia Fallon, *Hidden Sea*

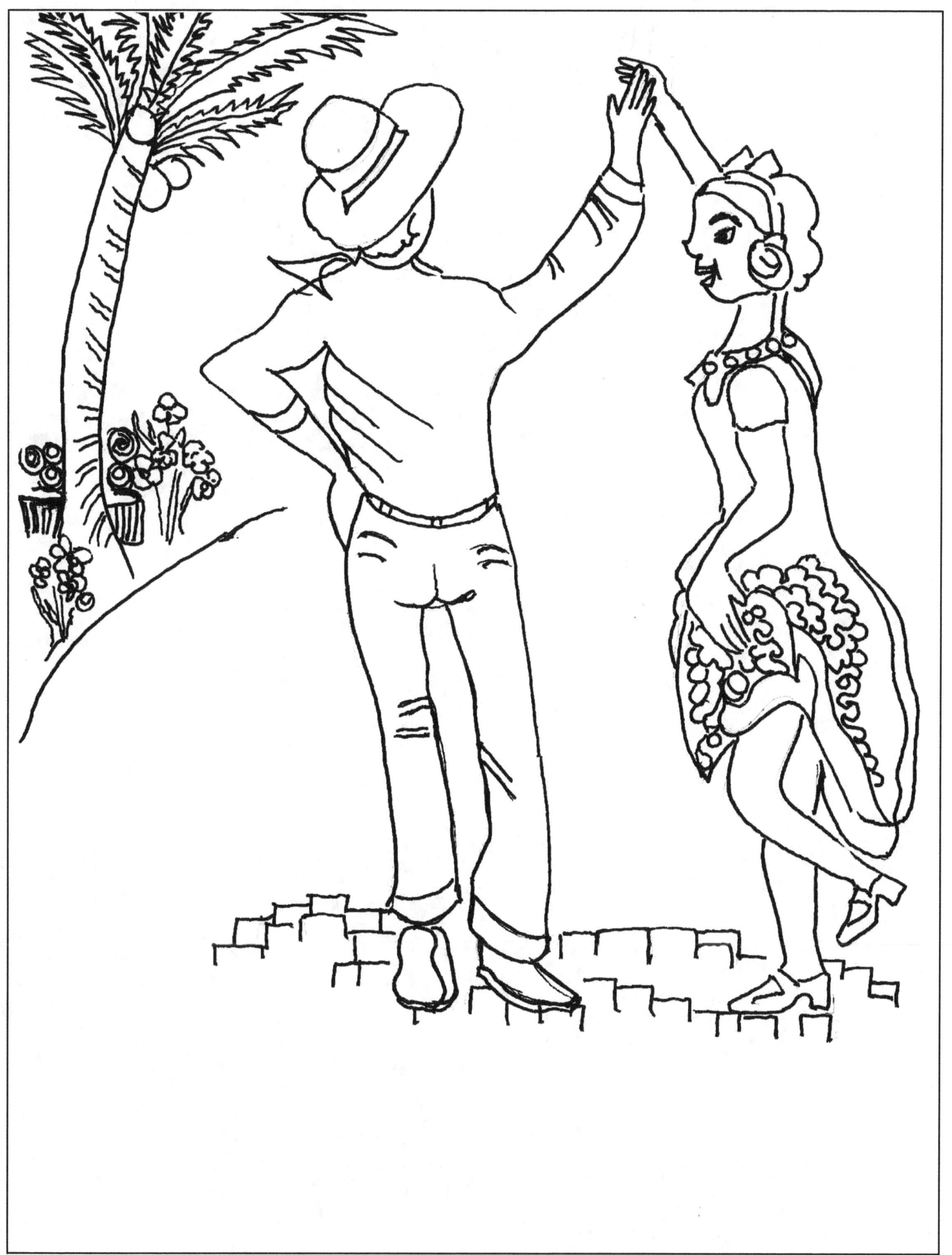

Larry Cardwell, *Dancers in Puerto Rico*

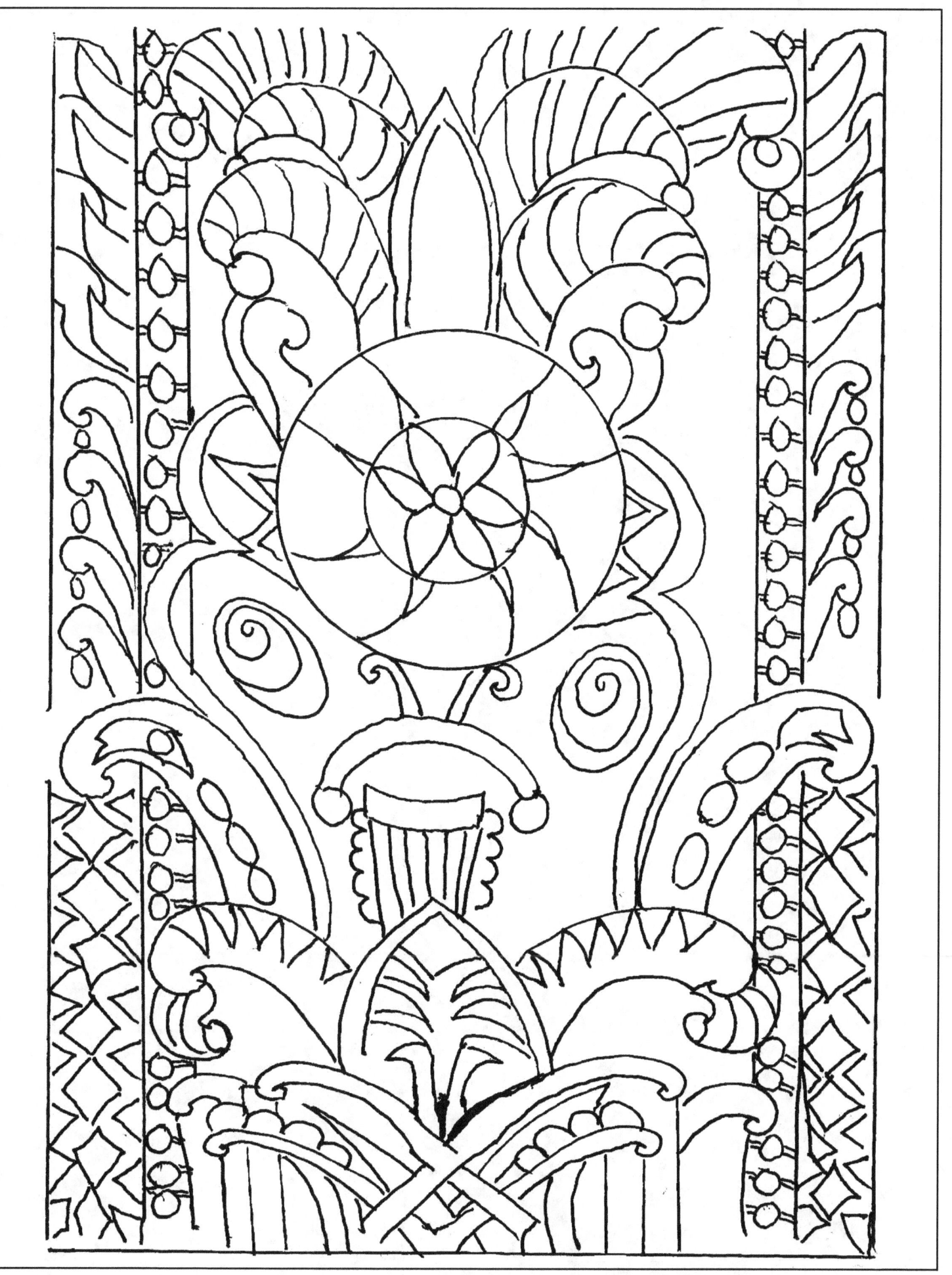

Ellen Cardwell, *Art Deco Design in Racine*

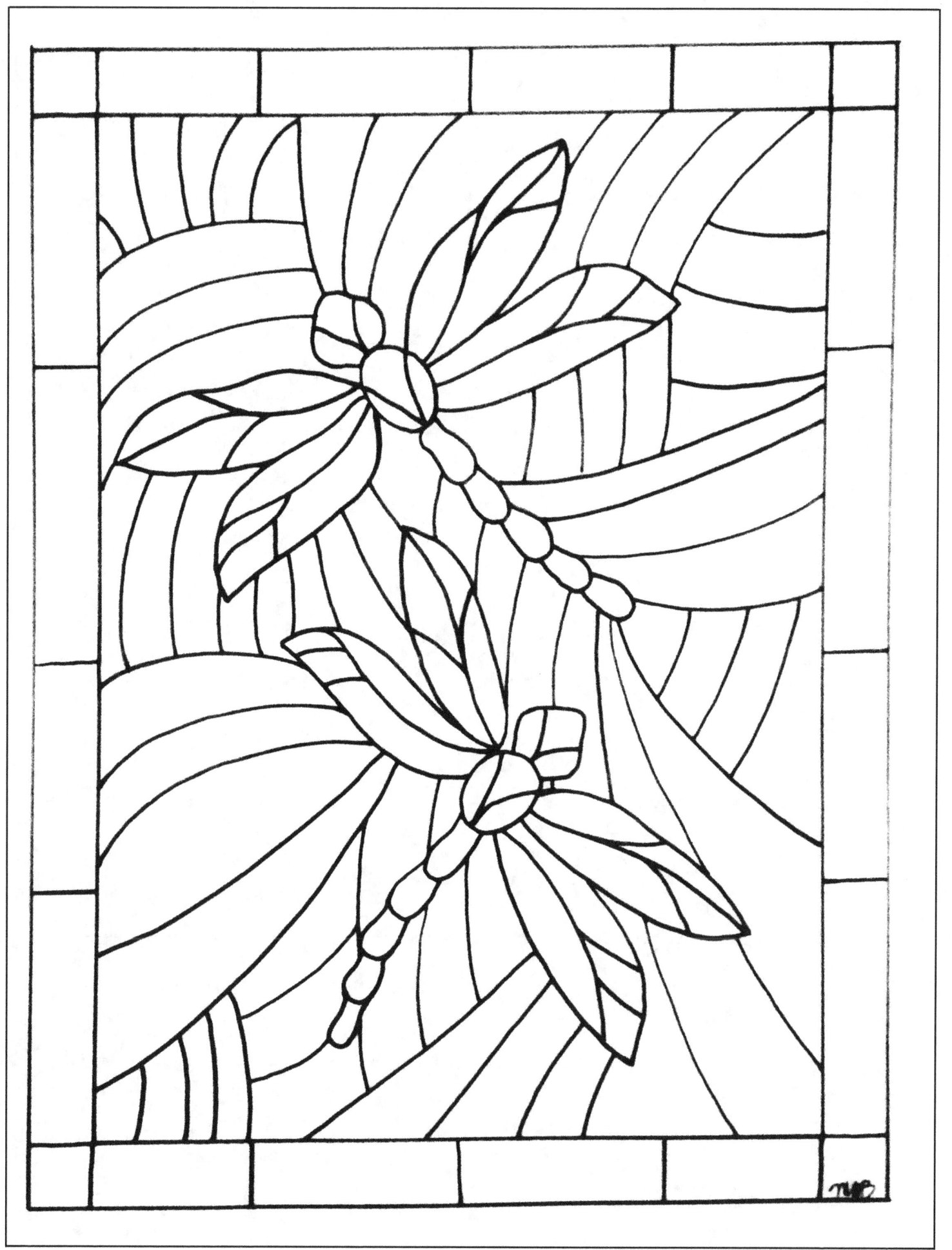

Mary Ann Breshnehan, *Dragonflies*

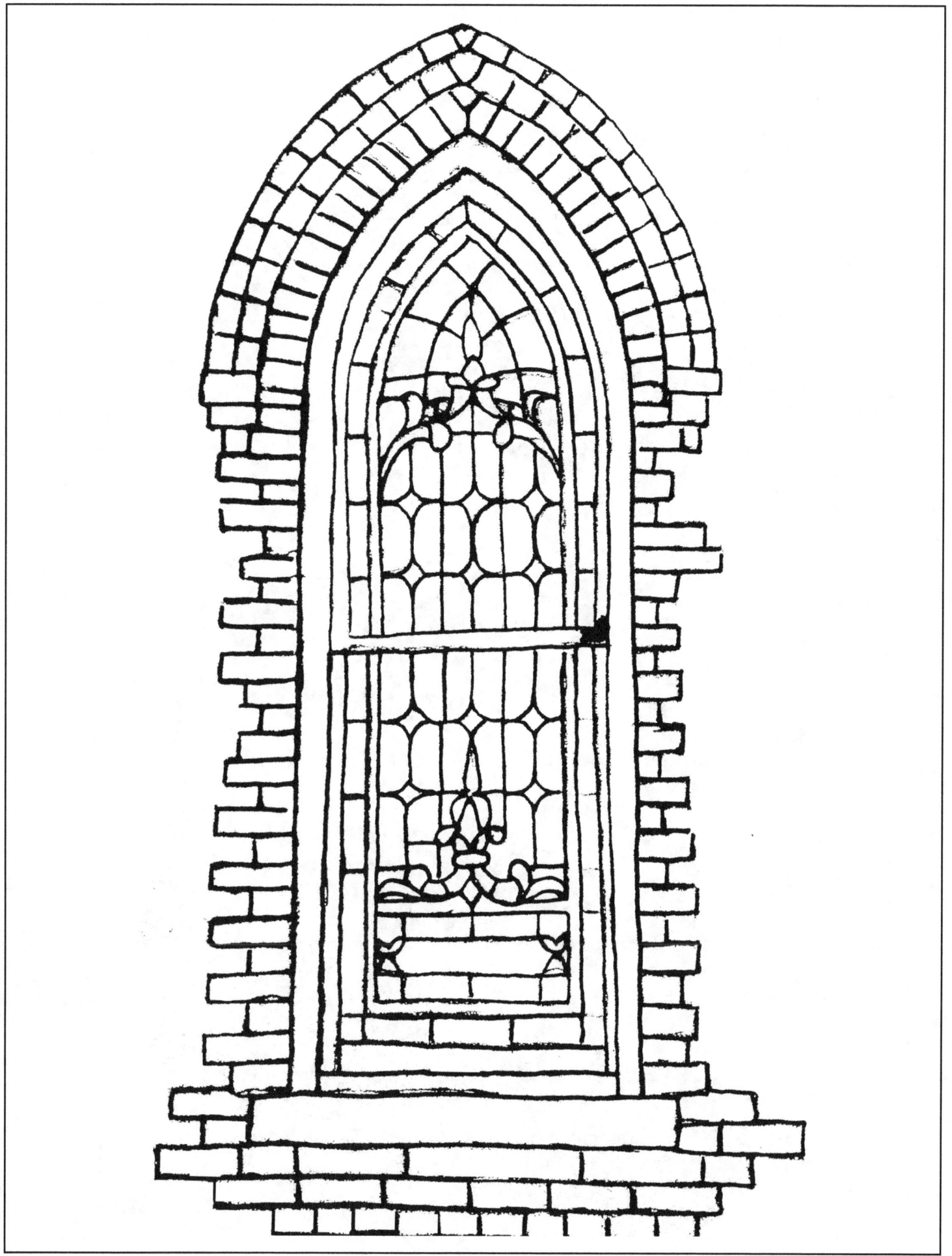

Kelly Steitz

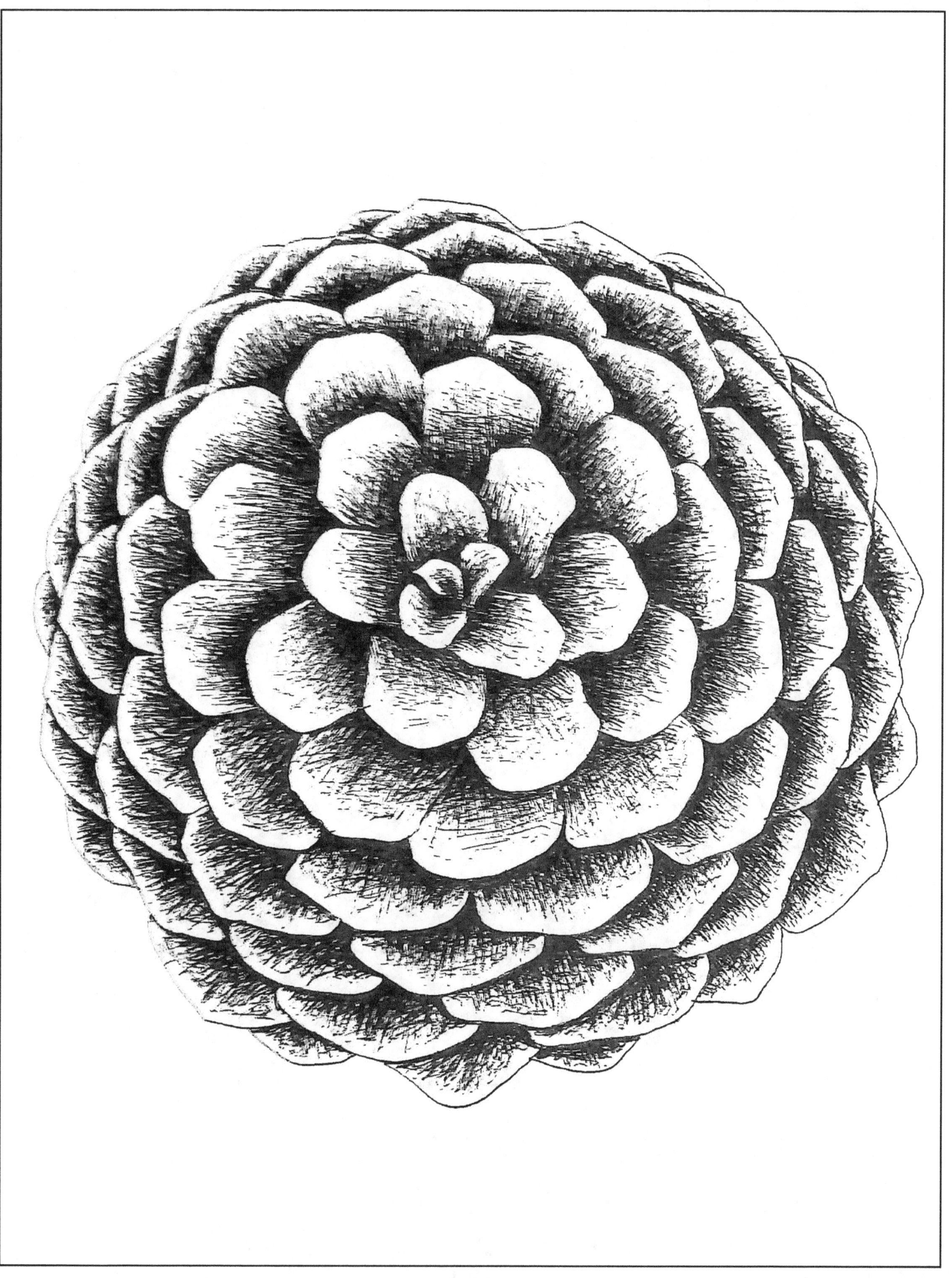

Jess LaFon Furlough, *Pinecone*

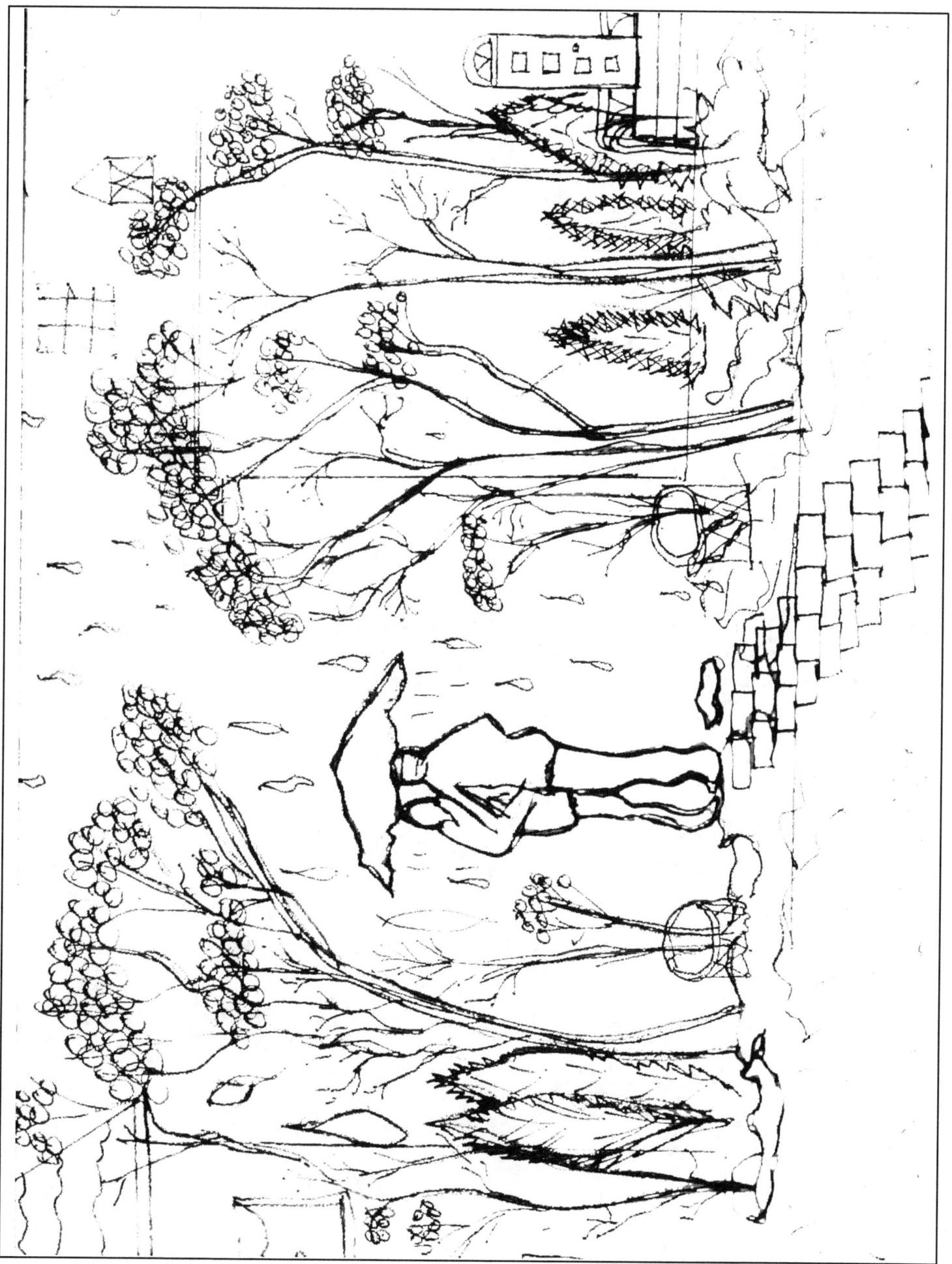

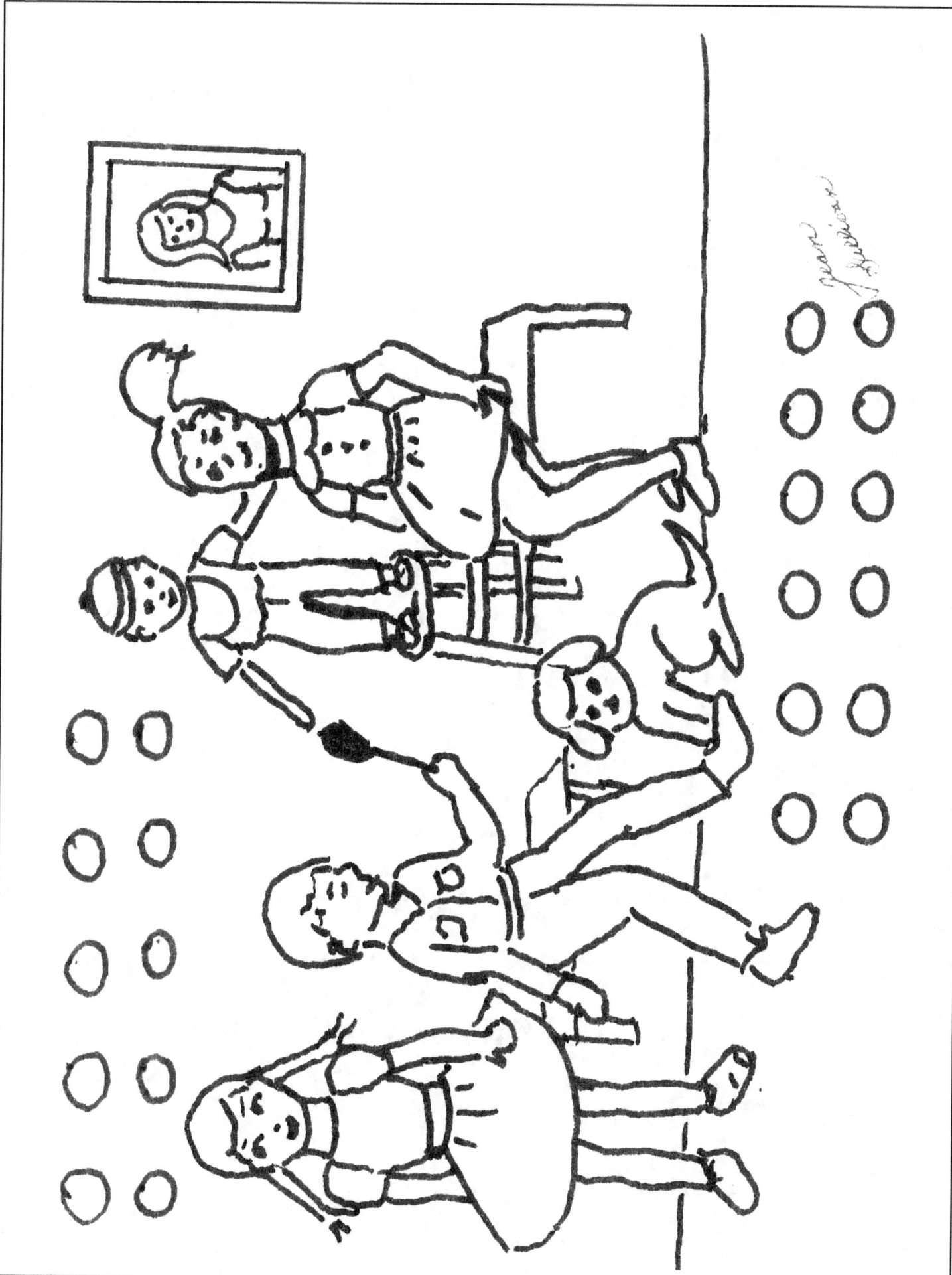

Charles A. Wustum Museum of Fine Arts

Janet Mrazek, *Wustum Museum*

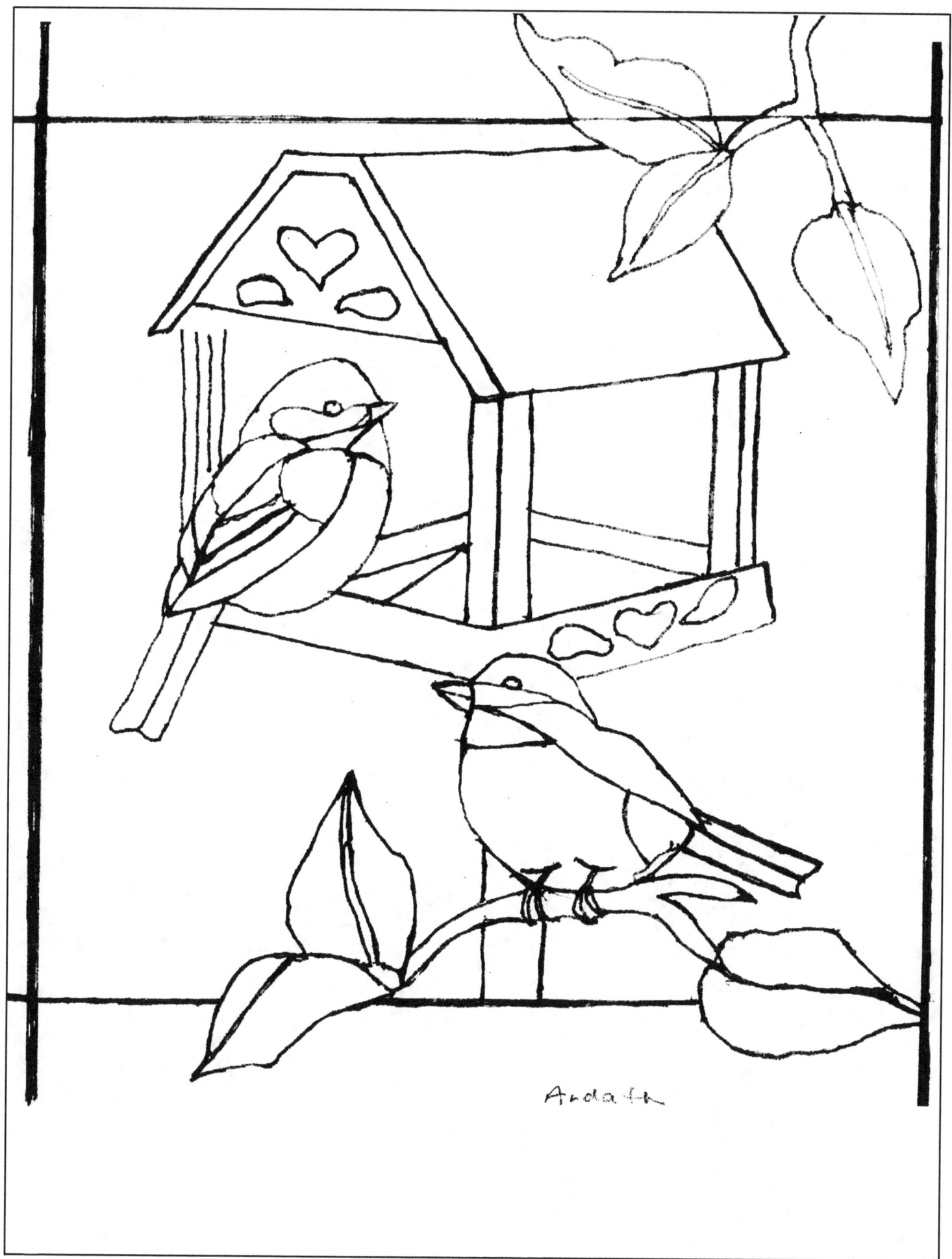

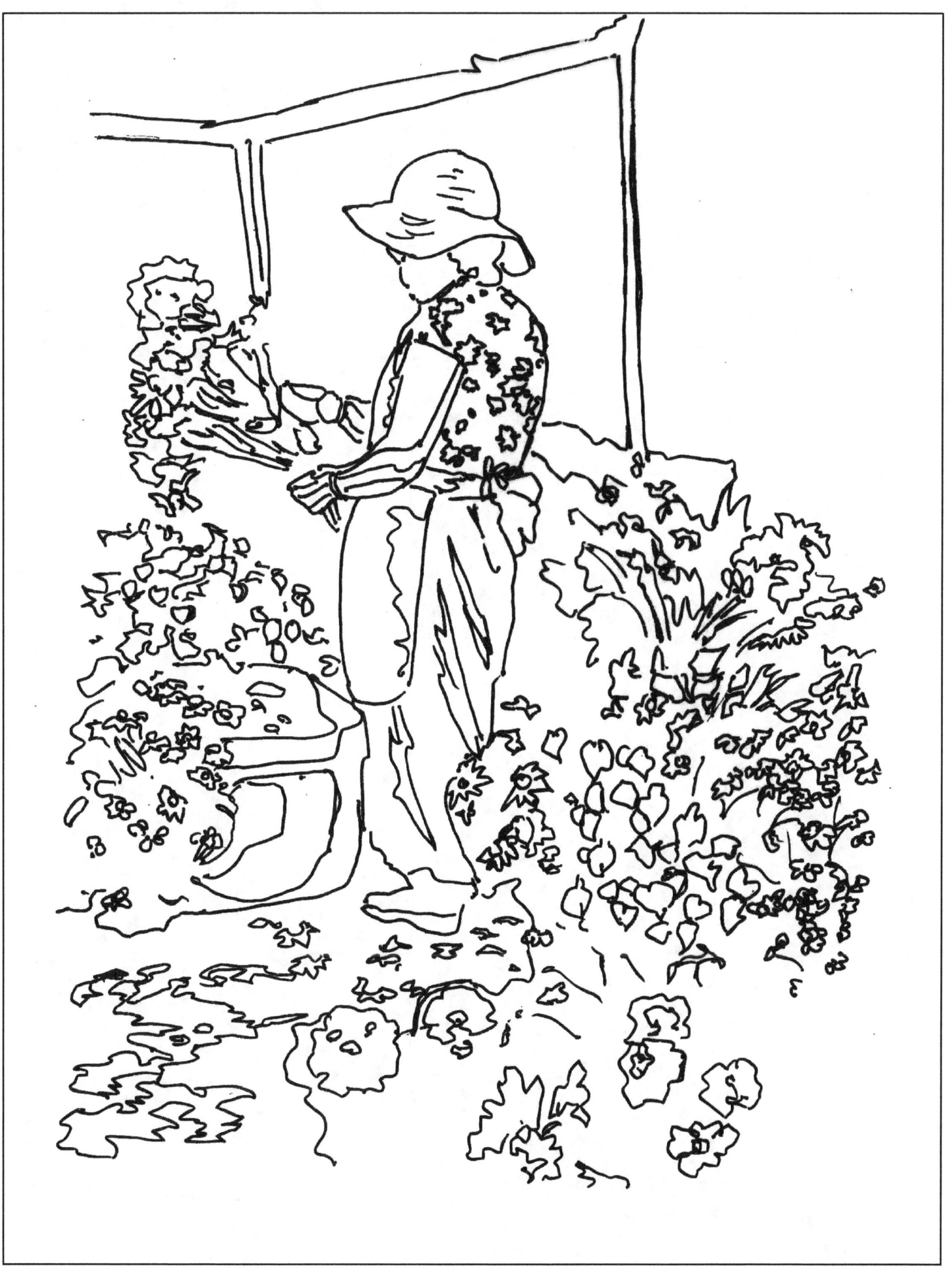

Carlotta Miller, *Choices*

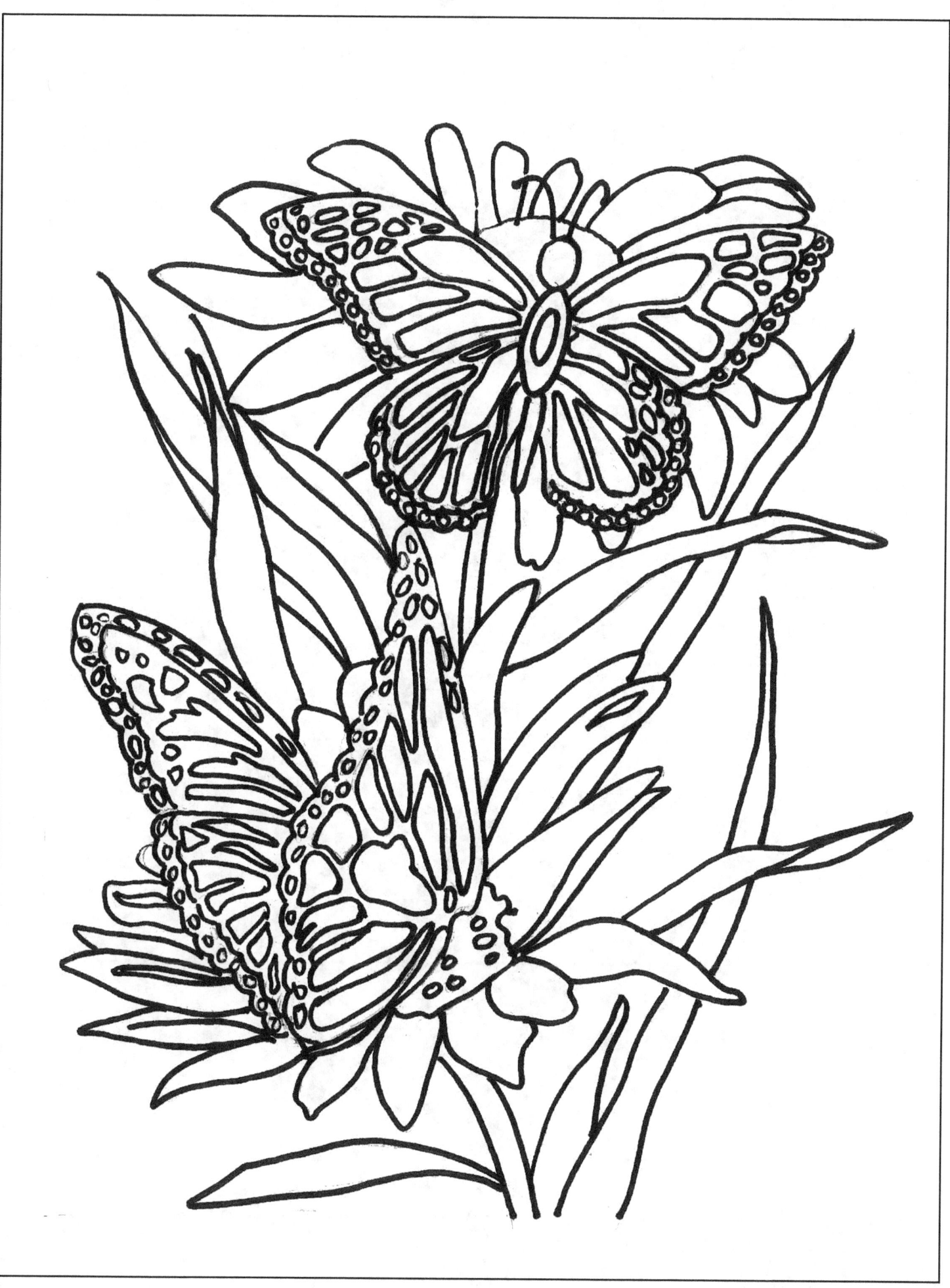

Janet Thompson, *Butterflies*

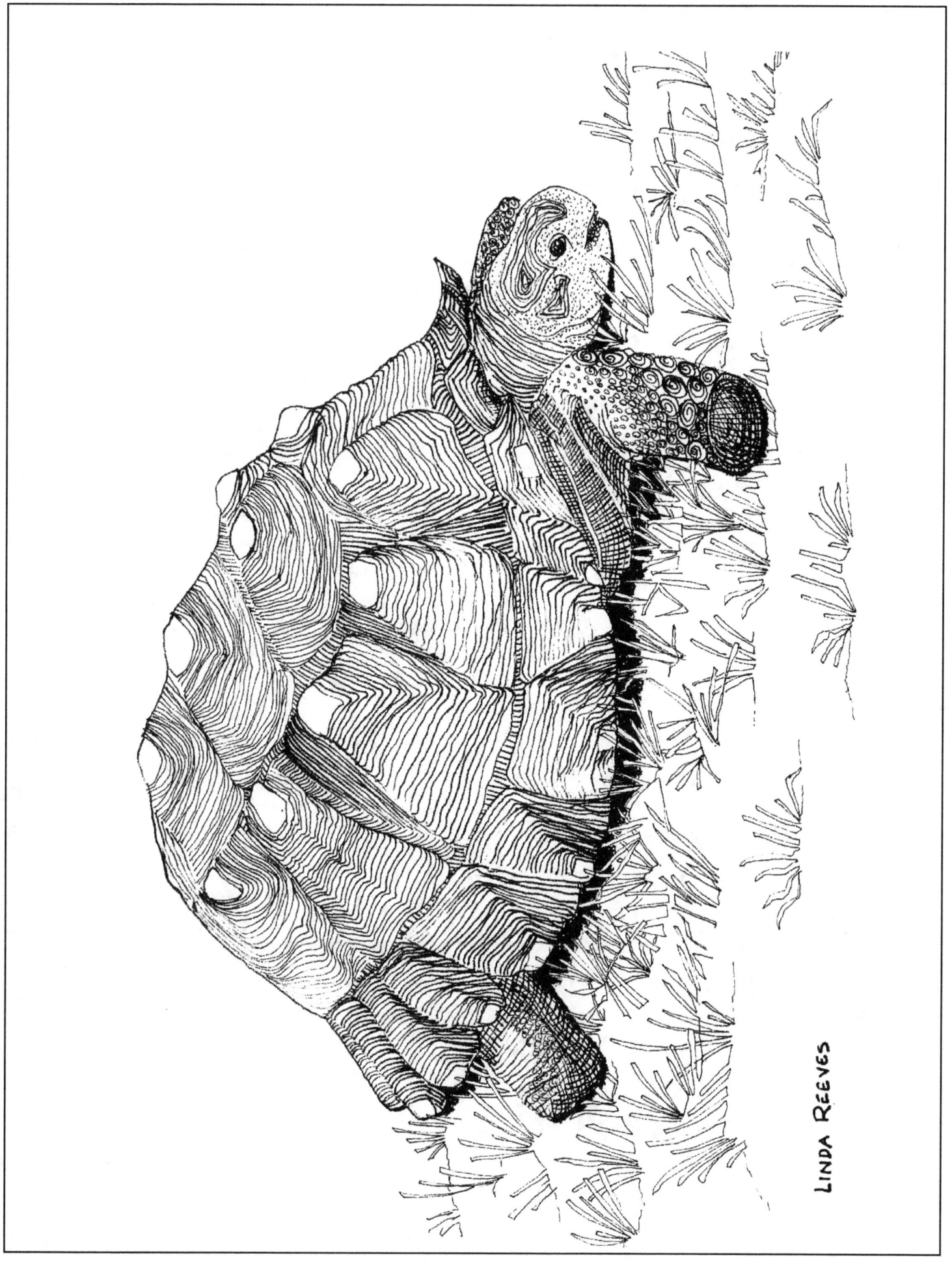

LINDA REEVES

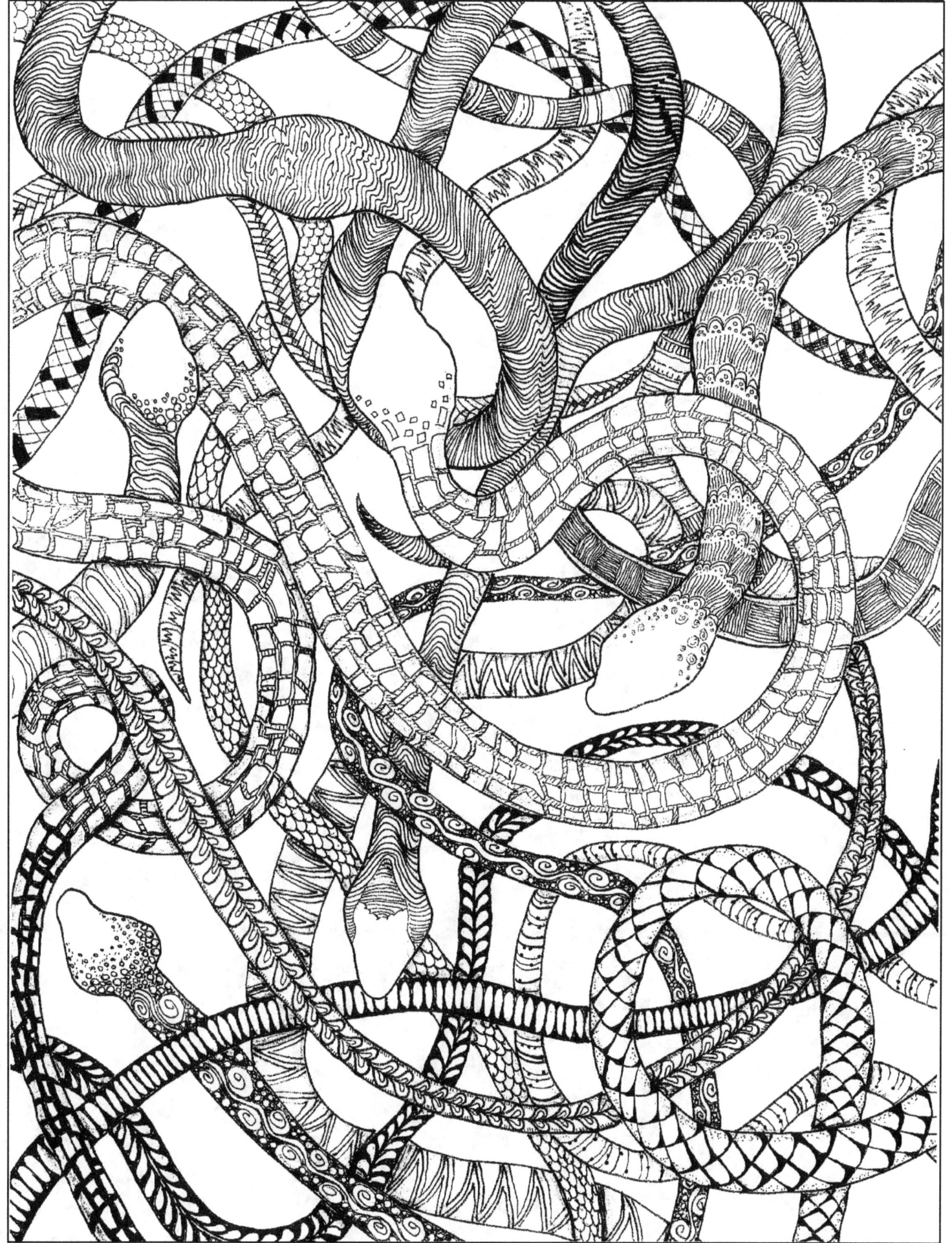

Linda Reeves

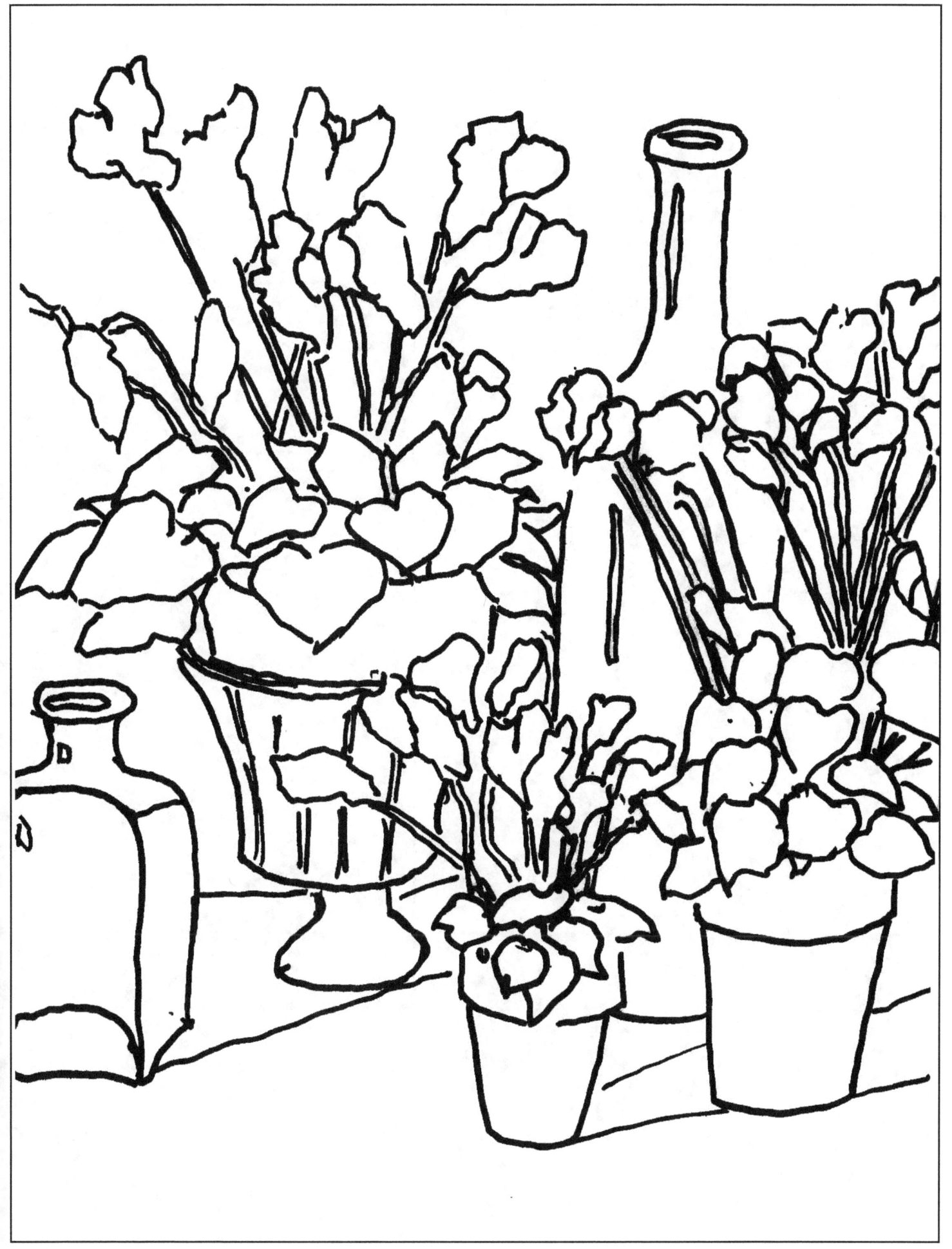

Nancy Neider

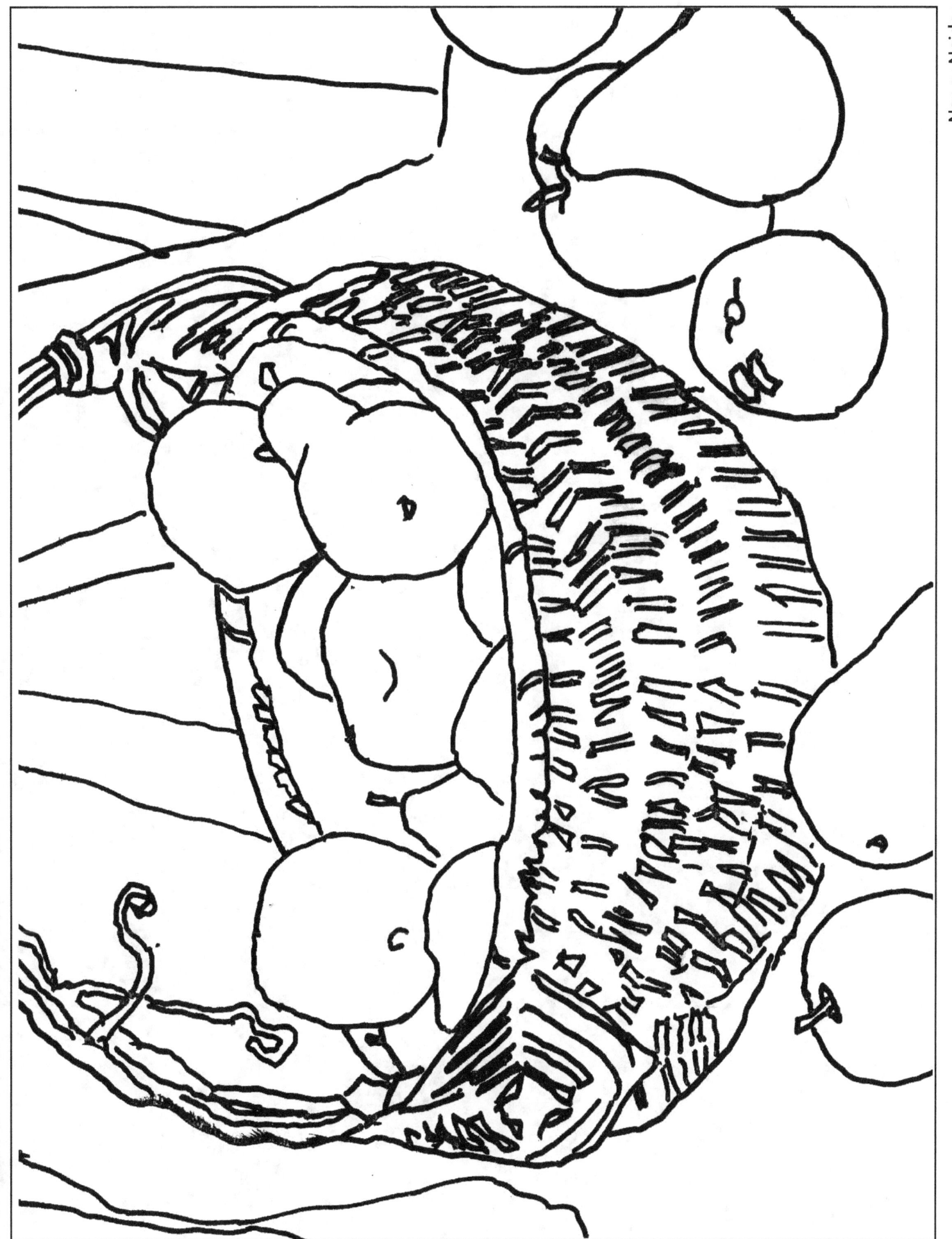

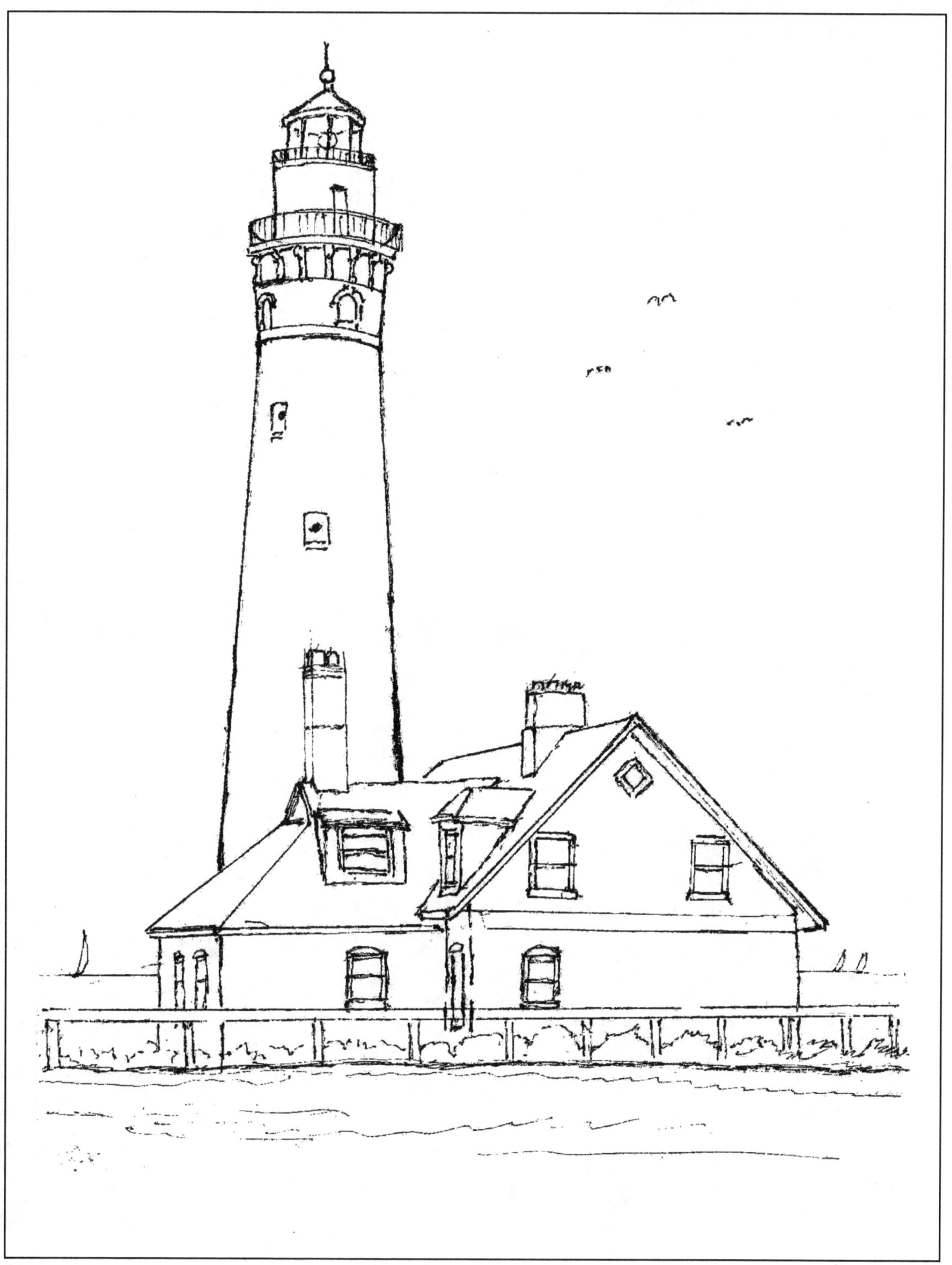

Don Vander Leest, *Wind Point Light House*

"Thank you to all who made this 50th Anniversary of Starving Artist Fair possible!"
Racine Art Guild Current Membership

Sarah & David Andersen
Taylor Bahr
Regina Baker
Beverly Becharas
Jerry & Dianne Belland
Jim Beyer
Barb Blaha
Christine Bohn
Russell Bohn
Cindy Bojcic
Mary Ann Bresnahan
Karen Broman
Ellen R. & Larry D. Cardwell
Jill Castillo
Jim Chaplin
Trace and Susan Chiodo
Caye Christensen
Nick & Geri Cibrario
John Clazmer
Martha Coaty
Linda Pierangeli Davis
Terry Dennis
Helen Douglas
DeeDee Dumont
Mary Dwyer
John Falk
Wesley & Patricia Fallon
Barb Farrell
Lydia Fervoy
Jessica Lafon Furlough
Anne Frontier
David Gaura
Samira Gdisis
Pat Gilbert
Cindy Goffe
Janis Gorski
Nancy Greenebaum

Alexander Greiveldinger
Pat Guttenberg
Ryen and Jasper Hagemann
Diane Hamlin
Phyllis Heinen
Ann Henkes
Janet Hoffman
Tom Hoffman
Candace Hoffmann
Cathleen Holmes
Sue Horton
Kathy Hueffner
Sande Jensen
Nancy Justus
Sue Kadamian
Pam Kazarian
Lisa KC
Kathleen Knutell
Christopher Koontz
Georgia Kroll
Mickie Krueger
Susan Manalli
Carol Madsen
Lisa Martin
Tanja Martinez
Karen Mathis
Marilyn McGoldrick
Carlotta Miller
Christine Miller
Mary (Poetschke) Mollerskov
Janet Mrazek
Corinne Multhauf
Nancy Neider
Mary Nelson
JoAnne Nissen
Richard Nondahl
Joyce Ottum

Lyle & Laurel Peters
Thom & Dorie Petersen
Julie Peterson
Kate Peterson
Pat Pilling
H. June Pomatto
Lance Raichert
Linda Reeves
Suzanne Schackelman
Mary A. Schall / Yvonne Stevenson
Brenda Schuls
Sue Smith
Harold & Lois Solberg
Lee Sorensen
Judith Stalder
Kelly Steitz
Jean Sullivan
Ginny Sullivan
Jean Tenuta
Mary Terselic
Jean Thielen
Brenda & Ronald Thomas
Janet Thompson
Don Tobias
Ardath J. Trebra
Paula Touhey
Greg Uttech
Joe Van Hulle
Don Vander Leest
Rebecca Venn
Donald and Eileen Voss
Krysta Voss
Dina Walker
Sherri Wistrom
Marc Wollman